A Guide to...
Gouldian Finches
Their Management, Care & Breeding

By John Sammut & Dr Rob Marshall

Published and Edited by ABK Publications ©

© **1991 Australian Birdkeeper**

All rights reserved. No part of this publication may be reproduced, stored in any retrieval system, or transmitted in any form or by any means without the prior permission in writing of the publisher.

**First Published 1991 by
Australian Birdkeeper
PO Box 6288,
South Tweed Heads,
NSW. 2486. Australia.
First Reprint 1992**

ISBN 0 9587455 6 0

Front Cover:
Top left: Red-headed Gouldian. (Peter McGrath)
Ctr left: Black-headed Gouldian Cock. (Wilson Moore)
Btm left: Single factor Yellow-backed Cock (left) and Normal Cock. (Wilson Moore)
Right: Yellow-headed Lilac over White-breasted Blue-backed Cock. (Wilson Moore)

Back Cover:
Yellow-headed Cock. (Wilson Moore)

Page 7 - Yellow-headed Cock. (Wilson Moore)
Page 31 - A Black-headed hen. (Wilson Moore)
Page 55 - Red-headed cock. (Wilson Moore)

PROUDLY PUBLISHED & PRINTED IN AUSTRALIA

Contents

About the Authors/Acknowledgements .... Page 4
Introduction .... Page 5
Management .... Page 7
   The Aviary .... Page 8
   Lighting; Heat; Other methods of housing Gouldians; Cage breeding.
   Furniture and Utensils .... Page 12
   Nest boxes; Food and water containers; Soft food container; Cuttlefish bone clips; Grit container; Green food container; Seed cleaners; Seed winnowers.
   Buying, Transporting &
   Settling Newly Acquired Birds .... Page 14
   Travelling; Settling and quarantining new arrivals.
   Nutrition .... Page 15
   Carbohydrates; Fats; Proteins; vitamins; Minerals; Water; Grit; The Gouldian diet that I have found to be successful; Sprouting seeds.
   The Annual Dietary
   Requirements of the Gouldian .... Page 18
   Moulting season; Non breeding season.
   Breeding Gouldian Finches .... Page 19
   Breeding season; Colony breeding; Courtship behaviour; Producing eggs; hatching and rearing them; Keeping breeding records and ringing birds; Failure to breed; Using Bengalese as foster parents; The Bengalese finch; Bengalese set up; Fostering; Imprinting.
Mutations and Colour Breeding .... Page 29
   Head Colours in the Gouldian Finch .... Page 30
   Mutations .... Page 35
The Health of the Gouldian Finch .... Page 47
   Health aspects of the newly acquired Gouldian Finch; The causes of disease in the Gouldian Finch; Water hygiene; Food hygiene; Sprouting hygiene; Sprouting procedure; Food and water management; Disease related to bad hygiene in the aviary; Appropriate quarantine; Nutritional aspects of disease; Informed use of medications; Temperature control; Foster parents; The 'Carrier Bird'; Gouldians in a mixed aviary; Overcrowding; Recognition of disease; Transport the body to the veterinarian in a cooler; Prevention of disease in the Gouldian aviary; Disease prevention in the off season; Disease prevention for the breeding season; Disease prevention during the adult moulting season; Medication after the adult moult; Disease prevention during the juvenile moult; Preventative programme for fledgings; The more common diseases seen in the Gouldian Finch; External parasites.
Publishers Note .... Page 88
   Including Bibliography

JOHN SAMMUT   DR ROB MARSHALL

About the Authors

John Sammut has always been interested in and fascinated by birds in one way or another from his earliest years. For the past ten years or so he has been concentrating all his efforts on the Gouldian Finch. John stresses that the path to understanding this most beautiful bird has really never been smooth or easy but he can state with a degree of confidence that his efforts in this regard have to date been encouraging and rewarding.

Dr Rob Marshall B.V.Sc. M.A.C.V.Sc. (Avian Health) has been keeping birds himself since 1960. He has been a practicing veterinarian with a special interest in birds since 1975. He has studied bird medicine in Germany, Holland and the United States of America. He has and still does lecture to bird groups in Australia and overseas. These include lectures to Avian Veterinarians in the USA in 1989 and 1990 at their international AAV Conferences. He writes regularly for magazines which include Australian Birdkeeper, Pigeon Fancier and The Pet Industry News. His special interest is in Racing Pigeons, Gouldian Finches and Golden-shouldered Parrots. Rob first became interested in the Gouldian Finch and all its problems over ten years ago while studying bird medicine in Germany.

It was about three years ago that John, seeking the advice of an avian veterinarian, met and developed a tremendous working relationship with Dr Rob Marshall which continues to this day.

Dr Rob Marshall's expertise in the field of avian medicine coupled with John Sammut's enthusiasm has enabled them to solve many of the problems with the Gouldian Finch. They have now approached the stage of knowing what is happening in the aviaries at any given time and why it is happening. The guess work which plagued Gouldian Finch management in the early years has all but disappeared and has been replaced with proven methods of practice.

No longer do they consider the Gouldian to be a sensitive finch but rather a finch whose special needs had perhaps not been satisfied in the past.

They are both very happy to be given this opportunity to share their knowledge and experience of this intriguing bird with the avicultural world.

Acknowledgements

The authors would like to thank Ray and Wendy Lowe, Don Crawford and Wilson Moore for their contributions to the chapter on Colour Mutations and Colour Breeding.

Introduction

In 1884 John Gould placed it in the genus *Amadina* thinking that the Gouldian Finch was related to the Cutthroat Finch and other African species. This concept is no longer held.

In 1862 Reichenback said this genus should be called *Chloeba*.

In 1943 Dr Jean Delacour (Zoologica, 1943 Vol. 28) agreeing with earlier ornithologists, included it in the genus *Poephila* arguing that the Gouldian Finch resembles the Grass Finches, because of long tail feathers and similarities in the shape of wings and beaks. According to Klaus Immelmann (Australian Finches in Bush and Aviary, 1965) the characters used for placing the Gouldian Finch in the genus *Poephila* (shape of tail and drinking in a pigeon-like manner) are mere adaptations. These adaptations have developed several times independently within the family of Grass Finches.

Immelmann and others ... Butler (as early as 1899) Neunzig, Wolters, Steiner and Mitchell all agree that the Gouldian Finch resembles the Parrot Finch (genus *Erythrura*) ... general colouration, head colours pattern, nesting in holes in the wild, nodules on the side of the mouth in nestlings etc. There are also similarities between the Gouldian Finch and the Mannikins (genus *Lonchura*). These similarities have been pointed out in detail by Mrs F M Hall (Symposium for the Zoological Society of London, 1962).

Immelmann and Mr Derek Goodwin (Estrildid Finches of the World, 1982) both argue that while its relationship to other genera is unknown it seems best to place the Gouldian Finch in a separate genus for itself. In this case *Chloebia* (Reichenbach 1862) is the oldest name available and it is probably the most widely accepted and used by authorities to describe the Gouldian Finch.

But the purpose of this exercise is not to argue whether the generic name *Chloebia* is right or wrong. The experts will determine that for us. The purpose of this exercise is to generate enough interest amongst aviculturists to work hard with this species. Field work is needed to determine why the Gouldian Finch is declining so rapidly in the wild. Aviculturists must continue to learn, develop and improve breeding methods so that, come what may, the Gouldian Finch will at least survive as a cage and aviary bird.

Dr Sonia Tideman, research scientist with the Conservation Commission of the Northern Territory is working towards solving the reason for the Gouldian Finches decline in the wild. Dr Tideman suggests whilst it is true that air-sac mite seems to be a likely cause of the decline of the Gouldian Finch, the problem is that at present not enough is known to rule out other causes of population decline, such as habitat destruction by fire, pastoral activities and other man-associated effects, shortage of food, breeding sites or mates, illegal trapping and disease and so on.

In 1989 Dr Tidemamn said "We are proceeding as rapidly as we can to provide more concrete evidence for the decline of the Gouldian Finch, but with a very rare bird this takes time ... at least another three years".

Today we are beginning to see dedicated aviculturists endeavouring to improve the breeding methods. The importance of creating conditions in captivity similar to those in the wild cannot be overstressed. The bird may not be as much of a "problem bird" as it was in the past but there is still much to be learnt, and while the Gouldian is not a "beginner's" finch, experienced aviculturists should be able to cater for its needs.

The following five chapters are an account of my experience with the Gouldian Finch over a period of ten years. Some readers may agree with the following account whilst others may disagree. If that is the case then my aim will have been achieved, because it is only through debate and discussion that the methodology of Gouldian Finch breeding in captivity will improve.

1 - DR ROB MARSHALL

1 - John Sammut's aviaries in Sydney

Management

The Aviary

I have always bred Gouldians in box type aviaries. In Sydney I have seen them housed in a variety of ways, but I feel it is correct to say that the most successful Gouldian breeders are those who use the (preferably) fully enclosed box type aviary attached to a flight.

1 - DR ROB MARSHALL

2 - DR ROB MARSHALL

1 - John Sammut's aviaries in Sydney

2 - Galvanised fittings are an alternative to welding pipe together

Ideally aviaries, especially Gouldian aviaries, should face north if possible, so that the sun penetrates the front of the aviary in winter until late in the afternoon and the extra warmth will benefit the birds that are generally breeding at that time.

The type of aviary I use is just over 3 metres (9ft 6in) long by approximately 1 metre (3ft) wide and about 2.1 metres (6ft 8in) high. Half of the structure is fully enclosed while the other half is flight area. The enclosed section is fully insulated and lined. The aviary rests on brick footings which rise about 150mm (6in) above ground level. Thin-walled galvanised pipes held together

1 - DR ROB MARSHALL

2 - DR ROB MARSHALL

1 - A side view through the flights
2 - The back of the aviaries. The top section is opened for inspection or extra ventilation if necessary. The middle section provides access to the feed table and the lower door allows entry into the shelter.

with pipe fittings were used to build the flight section. Special attention was given when covering the flight area with thick gauge 1/2 by 1/2 inch galvanised mesh in order to keep rodents and mice out. The front of the enclosed section has a flap door which is the full width of the aviary and about 500mm (1ft 6in) high. When this flap is down the aviary is fully enclosed. Just beneath the flap door is an opaque glassed area 700mm (2ft 4in) high. Clear glass is not an ideal medium as birds injure themselves trying to fly through it. The back of the aviary has a low entrance door. Above it a small door opens onto a feeding platform. Feeding and watering is done through this small door and the only time I enter the aviary is at cleaning time. Above this and at eye level, an inspection flap type door is installed, so that birds are able to be checked whenever necessary without causing them undue stress. On the opposite side and 250mm (9in) from the ceiling is another shelf which is partitioned into three compartments. At the beginning of the breeding season, I place a breeding box in each compartment, thereby isolating breeding pairs from each other. This method minimises the infighting which generally takes place while they are settling down. At the end of the breeding season the shelf is boarded up and the aviary is then used to colour-up young birds which have been in holding cages until then. The floor of the enclosed section is concrete. Upon this a thick sheet of plastic is laid to eliminate dampness and on top of this several layers of paper sheeting is laid and once a week the top layer is taken off. That way droppings, husks and food remains which might otherwise attract undesirables are removed regularly.

Lighting

There is no denying that winter days are short of daylight and as Gouldians breed well into winter some form of artificial lighting is in order and I believe essential when young are in the nest and being reared. The provision of a fluorescent light so that daylight can be increased during the short days of winter can only improve the survival chances of newly hatched birds, by allowing their parents to continue feeding well into the evening. A minimum of fourteen hours of daylight is ideal for the survival and healthy upbringing of young birds. Daylight should be controlled by an auto time switch. In my aviaries light comes on at 5am and is switched off at 8pm. It is advisable to provide a second source of lighting in the form of a low intensity (I use a 15w pilot globe) night light. The night light, which is also on an auto switch, can be adjusted to come on fifteen minutes before the daylight switches itself off. That way the birds are prevented from being plunged suddenly into darkness. The dim light also reduces the chances of birds injuring themselves in the event of a night fright.

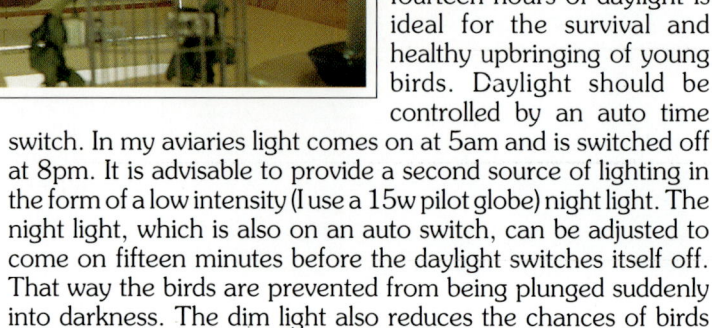

Heat

Where I live in Sydney the temperature in winter plunges well below 10 degrees C night after night, and on many occasions it barely goes above 13 degrees C day after day. The correct temperature at which Gouldians should be kept is always vigorously debated, but suffice to say that if we are going to emulate the conditions of their natural habitat, then the Sydney winter is, to say the least, somewhat colder than that which they should be subjected to. Birds bred locally appear to tolerate the winter rather well, but temperatures below 13 degrees C for prolonged periods of time will affect their general condition and

1 - A view of the elevated feed table inside the back door
2 - A view from the back door, over the feed table showing the heater and lights. The access door to the flight is closed.

their breeding performance will suffer as a result. This condition comes about because the birds are utilising a considerable amount of energy in maintaining their body heat.

Of course one could argue that the objectives of true aviculturists should be to develop a hardy strain of Gouldian which can live and breed well outside its natural environment.

However as aviculturists we should remind ourselves that we cannot remake the Gouldian Finch to suit cold climates by wishing the bird had an undercoat!

My method is to maintain a temperature of 18-20 degrees C by using a thermostatically controlled heater. In this way I have consistently and successfully reared a good number of Gouldians every year.

Other Methods of Housing Gouldians

Half Open Type Aviary

Another method of housing Gouldians and one which seems to produce better results the farther north one breeds, is the half-flight, half-shed type aviary. Breeders in Queensland use this type of aviary with greater success than breeders using the same type of aviary in the southern States. The northern climate is more conducive to breeding the Gouldian Finch as it is closer to the birds' natural environment. With this type of aviary one has no control in maintaining a steady and uniform temperature in winter, but is it necessary in Queensland where the climate is milder and much more agreeable to the bird than that of the southern States?

The Gouldian has a habit of camping out in the flight area during the night and seems reluctant to use the shelter provided. This does not present a problem to the Queensland breeder but it would to the southern State breeders. In winter when the temperature is low, the bird is burning up energy trying to maintain body warmth. This in turn must affect its general condition, not to mention its breeding performance.

Open Type Aviary

This type of aviary is essentially a large flight with a partly covered roof or sometimes no cover at all. This is not suitable for Gouldian breeding. Such an aviary offers no shelter from winds and rain. Eliminating draughts in this type of aviary is impossible and the breeding results, if any, will be poor and discouraging, not to mention the havoc caused when predators such as butcher birds or cats are on the aviary.

Ornamental Aviary

This type of aviary is excellent to show off ones birds. The ornamental aviary is generally built to enhance the appearance of a garden and but is not practical when it is required to be used for breeding purposes.

It is important to remember that the main essential in keeping and breeding Gouldians is an aviary which is comfortable and **draught free**. Gouldians are very susceptible to draughts.

Cage Breeding

In Australia breeding Gouldians in cages is not widely practiced. The weather by and large is favourable and building an aviary in a backyard is easier and cheaper than building a bird room for cage breeding.

However, if the aim of the aviculturist is to improve the quality and standard of the Gouldian Finch then selective breeding is essential.

The size of the cage is of no great importance, as long as the birds feel secure. For this reason I recommend a box type cage with a wire front at least 450mm (1ft 4in) deep. Height and width could be varied but I feel that 900mm (3ft) long and 600mm (2ft) high is enough room for a pair of birds. I have seen Gouldians bred in smaller cages just as successfully. Two perches are placed as far apart from each other as possible, but not too close to the ends of the cage otherwise the cock's tail feathers will be damaged. Some breeders place the perches diagonally opposite each other. They maintain such an arrangement gives the birds more exercise by making them fly up to the top perch. Perches are 10mm thick and are roughened up by dragging a fine toothed saw along them. The wire front must have all the openings to accommodate a nest box, seed and water containers, soft food container, a clip to hold the cuttlefish bone and an opening sufficiently large enough to catch the birds. A small net 150-200mm (approx. 6in) in diameter comes in very handy. A container with mineralised grit hung on the inside of the cage front will complete the set up.

Furniture and Utensils

Nest Boxes

Ply boxes are 130mm (5in) cube with an opening approximately one third of the box's height and a small landing perch 25mm below the opening.

1 - The open fronted nest box favoured by the author.

1 - DR ROB MARSHALL

Food and Water Containers

It is of utmost importance that the food and water containers be prevented from becoming fouled by droppings. For this reason water tubes or fonts, which could also be used for feeding are preferred to open dishes. The floor area of a cage is small and the likelihood of fouling open dishes is greater. These fonts when

1 - Fonts are less easily soiled than open dishes.
2 - Dishes such as these are ideal for soft food.

used for seed could easily be blocked if the seed is infested with web moth so care must be taken and the fonts checked regularly.

1 - DR ROB MARSHALL

Eranol$^{(T)}$, when used according to the manufacturer's instructions is most effective in eliminating the web moth, insects and their eggs from dry seed and is safe to use.

Soft Food Container

Budgerigar showcage drinkers are ideal containers because they hold enough soft food for parents and babies.

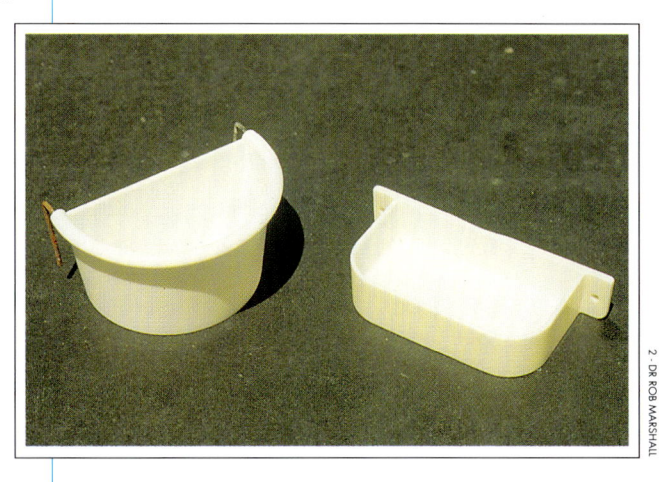

2 - DR ROB MARSHALL

Cuttlefish Bone Clips

The clips are used to hold a piece of cuttlefish bone on to the inside of the cage front. They look much nicer than multi coloured clothes pegs!

Grit Container

Grit is provided in a half moon shaped type dish which can be hooked onto the inside of the cage front..

Green Food Container

This container usually used for nest material makes an ideal green food receptacle.

Page 13

Seed Cleaners

A seed cleaner is most effective when used in conjunction with a vacuum cleaner to eliminate dust found in supposedly "dust free" seed.

Seed Winnowers

Home made seed winnowers used in conjunction with a vacuum cleaner separate husks from the uneaten seed. It is not recommended to feed the recycled uneaten seed to Gouldians because of the added health risk.

Buying, Transporting and Settling Newly Acquired Birds

Having set up the aviary it is time to purchase stock.

Though Gouldians are not difficult to maintain in the right conditions, they succumb very easily if subjected to inferior conditions.

I feel the best birds to buy when starting out are juveniles that have just come out of the moult and are raring to go. Gouldian Finches are readily obtainable from around November onwards but good quality birds are harder to come by. Preferably, Gouldians should be bought from a breeder who specialises in the species. Good stock is always in great demand and sometimes one has to wait until it becomes available. But it is well worth remembering that good stock is neither harder to maintain nor dearer to keep and with such birds there is a greater chance of keeping them in good condition and breeding them successfully.

No serious breeder should object to a prospective purchaser handling the birds he/she intends buying. When handling a bird check that the vent is clean and that it is full around the breastbone. Birds that have a sharp protruding breastbone are best left alone. Hand it back to the breeder for return to the aviary as it is likely the bird is unwell and may be "going light". Going light is a symptom and not a disease and a bird could be going light for several reasons. Other things to check for are breathing problems, feather quality, colour of feather, wet eye, colour of

1 - This type of container is ideal for holding green food or nesting material.

Travelling

skin (pale), skin health (plain and smooth and not flakey) and if possible its droppings.

Gouldians are poor travellers and become very distressed especially when travelling over long distances. To minimise distress a proper carrying box should be used. A box with a hinged or sliding front is ideal for carrying Gouldians as long as sufficient ventilation is provided. Small boxes are preferred to larger ones, because the birds are less likely to injure themselves if panicked. Overcrowding must be avoided. Supply a sprinkling of seed on the cage floor and if travelling over long distances, add to the cage a small plastic container with a piece of cotton wool soaked in water. By using soaked cotton wool attention to the birds drinking needs is met without messing the floor of the carrying cage.

As the car is invariably used to transport birds from A to B a few **do nots** are in order:

Do not transport your newly acquired and expensive Gouldians in the boot of the car. Exhaust fumes from the car will find its way into the boot with disastrous effects.

Do not leave the carrying cage in a locked car in the sun. Temperature rises very quickly in a locked-up car.

Do not put the carrying cage on the passenger seat as sudden braking will cause the box to tip over with possible injuries to its occupants.

Settling and Quarantining New Arrivals

Suppress your eagerness and do not put the birds in the aviaries. Instead, place them in holding cages for at least a fortnight, preferably three weeks. The birds' stress factor is going to be rather high until they get used to their new surroundings and as their resistance is low this is the time they are likely to get a bacterial infection. Put them onto a diet they have previously had and give them cooled boiled water for a few days. This will greatly eliminate their chance of contracting a bacterial infection. Introduce them to your diet and local water gradually. Have holding cages elevated with seed and water already in place. Have paper on the bottom of the cage to monitor droppings. Do not subject birds to any noise or disturbance and endeavour to keep them as warm as possible for the first few days. Make sure that seed and water is easily accessible. If the holding cage is large, scatter some seed and put a dish of water in the middle of the cage floor until there is no doubt in your mind that the birds have found their feeding and water stations.

At the end of the quarantine period I would suggest that one or two fresh droppings be taken to a vet who specialises in avian medicine for analysis.

Nutrition

Now we come to one aspect of bird keeping that must not be ignored by the aviculturist at any cost. It is the bird breeders duty to supply his birds with a balanced diet which will not only keep them healthy and vigorous but will permit the birds to breed successfully.

Birds in the wild have a variety of foods to choose from, but as it is impossible to supply captive Gouldians with the same foods then the aviculturist must find and supply suitable alternative foods.

A diet which includes carbohydrates, fats, proteins, vitamins, minerals and water is sufficient to provide for growth, development, reproduction and resistance to disease. A diet which is deficient in any one component puts the health of the bird at risk.

Carbohydrates

They provide the primary sources of energy to keep body warmth through their breakdown and supply energy to all the functioning parts of the birds body. It is almost impossible for a deficiency in carbohydrates to arise as Canary seed, French white, Japanese and Hungarian (Panicum) millets are very rich in carbohydrates.

Fats

These are also a source of energy but are not as easily digested as carbohydrates. Excess fats are stored in the body.

Proteins

Proteins are vital for the overall growth of the bird. Muscles, eyes, skin, feathers, nervous system etc all require protein for their proper development and growth. Proteins are made up of various amino acids and live insects such as mealworms and white ants and mashed hard boiled eggs are all excellent sources of amino acids.

Soaked and "just-sprouted" "oil" seeds eg niger and rape are rich in protein and carbohydrates while "starch" seeds eg canary and millets are rich in carbohydrates but lower in protein. When germinating seeds the starch is transformed into glucose and this in turn is more readily absorbed into the bird's digestive system.

Vitamins

Vitamins are required in only small amounts, nevertheless they are essential because a Vitamin A deficiency for example can cause sterility, retarded growth and blindness. Vitamin A deficiency in Gouldian Finches is very common. A lack of Vitamin D and Calcium (mineral) in adult Gouldians can cause soft-shelled eggs to be laid which could lead to egg binding. A diet which is perfect in every way but lacks one or more vitamins can only result in unhealthy birds.

Minerals

Minerals, like vitamins, are only required in very small amounts, nevertheless they are an essential part of the diet. For example, calcium is taken in great quantity by the egg-laying Gouldian hen for egg shell formation while phosphorus and calcium together are vital for bone formation.

Water

Water needs very little said about it except that it is the basis of all life and without it nothing survives. Clean water is essential. A vast number of diseases can be transmitted to the birds via their drinking water.

Grit

Grit has no nutritional value unless it is mineralised grit, in which case it has trace elements which are necessary for a completely balanced diet. Seed eating birds need grit to help digestion in the gizzard. Its function is to grind the food, mainly the seed which is swallowed whole, into smaller pieces. This will

The Gouldian diet that I have found to be successful

enable the digestive juices to act more effectively on the small pieces and the bird will gain greater benefit from its food.

In the non-breeding season when out of the moult I supply a dry mix which consists of 25% canary, 25% French white millet, 25% Japanese millet and 25% Hungarian (Panicum) millet, cuttlefish bone and mineralised grit. The above mix is always available and it forms the staple diet throughout the year. The four types of seeds fed are also very rich in carbohydrates. Vitamins are supplied in the water twice or three times weekly. Proprietary brands made for birds are readily available. Green food is also given about every second day. Birds in my aviaries are accustomed to endive and do not seem to be interested in anything else. Seeding grasses are highly nutritious if one can obtain them regularly. As I do not have a regular and constant supply of seeding grasses, I do not use them. Chickweed is another highly nutritious greenfood. The cultivation of your own seeding grasses and greenfood will ensure a regular, uncontaminated supply of greenfood.

During the breeding season they get all the above plus a soft food mix and sprouted seed once or twice daily depending if and how many youngsters are in the nest.

Some successful breeders give seeding grasses instead of soft food, others prefer sprouted seed, whilst others prefer more than one food.

Soft Food Mix I use:

My soft food mix is made up of the following ingredients:

1/2 cupful biscuit (as used by canary breeders or similar)

1 egg (boiled for a minimum of 20 minutes)

1/2 cupful of sprouts (just sprouted)

The egg is mashed and mixed with the ground biscuit then the sprouts are folded in.

The simpler the soft food formula the less problems one is likely to encounter. The soft food is prepared daily and if any is left over at the end of the day it is discarded and not refrigerated.

If the birds are not used to soft food keep persevering by offering it daily. Gouldians are very much creatures of habit and they do not take to new foods readily. One way of getting them to take a new food is to supply a teacher bird which is used to it. Another method, and one that I have found to work, is to place a new food at perch-height.

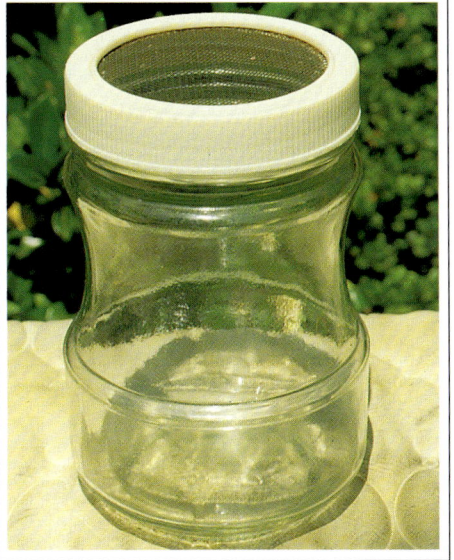

1 - Glass is superior to plastic to prevent disease in sprouted seeds.

Sprouting Seed

Seed sprouting starts when clean, fresh seed is placed in a container and water is added. A chemical change which transforms starch into glucose occurs during the sprouting process. The glucose provides an immediate source of energy for the rapidly growing babies. After twelve hours or so the water is drained and the seed washed thoroughly under running water. Drain the seed well and place in a warm place. An ideal place during winter is on top and towards the back of the refrigerator. Keep the seed moist by washing and draining morning and night, and when the sprouts appear, generally between the second and third day, the seed is ready to feed to the birds after being allowed to soak in a bleach solution for twelve minutes. Pour 25mls of ordinary household bleach into 2 litres of water and place seed in container for twelve minutes. Empty bleach solution and wash very thoroughly under running water, drain well, then it will be ready for use. The bleach will kill bacteria if present and I have used it for many years and find it to be very safe (More details on seed sprouting are given on page 57).

The Annual Dietary Requirements of the Gouldian.

Moulting Season

Juvenile birds start moulting at the age of 6-8 weeks. The process is a rather slow one taking some months. The juvenile Gouldian plumage is replaced in a progressive manner gradually revealing the adult colours. he feathers of the abdomen are the first to be replaced followed by those in the rump area. The breast patch begins to moult at about the same time as the head. The feathers on the back and wings are the last to be renewed followed by the pin feathers. Birds bred late in the season will not always moult completely and they get "stuck-in-the-moult" for the remainder of the year, however, these birds will moult successfully the following season. It does not always follow that birds which do not moult completely were bred late in the season.

1 - DR ROB MARSHALL

1 - Young White-breasted Yellow Gouldians in their juvenile moult.

A health set back eg. a bacterial infection due to overcrowding or lack of hygiene could also cause a bird to get "stuck-in-the moult".

Adult birds start moulting when the breeding season finishes. Shedding one coat of feathers and growing a new one poses an enormous drain on the birds' resources. This is a particularly stressful time and their resistance to bacterial infection is very low. Everything possible must be done to reduce stress and overcrowding the birds at this time will only produce more stress. Hygiene is very important at all times but more so during the moult. Soiled floors, aviary walls and perches all harbour bacteria, and should be cleaned regularly using Aviclens(T), Halamid(T) or similar. Food and water containers should be clean at all times and situated away from perches. Some breeders experience juvenile losses during the moult. Is it because an incorrect diet is supplied to the birds at this time? It is said feathers consist of about 90% protein. A diet rich in protein such as egg food and sprouted seeds should be supplied daily to the birds until the moult is complete.

I feel that losses would be greatly minimised if we do not overcrowd, maintain a high level of hygiene and supply the correct diet.

Non Breeding Season

After the birds have moulted the cocks are placed in one aviary and the hens in another away from each other and put on a seed only diet. It consists of 25% canary, 25% French white millet, 25% Japanese millet and 25% Hungarian millet. Vitamins, minerals and green food are supplied regularly, while cuttlefish and grit are on hand all the time. Highly nutritious foods like soft food, sprouted seeds, and seeding grasses are withheld. This time is referred to as the lean or austerity period. This period is similar to what the birds experience in the wild before the rains come. Food is not in abundance at this time. Cock Gouldians spend a lot of time singing. They attract quite an audience. The listening bird or birds perch very close to the singer, sometimes to the point where the singer has to lean away. This stance is known as peering and one gets the impression that the non-singing birds are listening very attentively. The audience may include cocks, hens and juvenile birds.

Breeding Gouldian Finches

Breeding Season

What appears to trigger the Gouldian to breed in the wild is the sudden flush of vegetation and an abundance of seeding grasses which soon appear after the rains. This change seems to awaken their reproductive organs into activity. In the cock it starts with the enlargement of testes which until now have been small and inactive. In the hen the ovaries begin to develop as she comes into breeding condition.

In captivity we trigger their breeding instinct by giving them a protein-rich diet such as egg food, sprouted seeds and/or seeding grasses.

The lean period finishes six weeks before the birds are paired and during this time the birds are brought into breeding condition by putting them on a protein-rich diet. Some breeders pair their birds in early December whilst others start late February depending on the climatic conditions. Breeders who use artificial lighting and heating can afford to pair their birds late. Under natural conditions breeding activities slow down with the onset of winter. However, birds which are under artificial lighting and heating do not appear to be affected by the onset of winter. The best time to set them up is when they are in top breeding condition. The birds should be bright and active and look as if they are raring to go - hens bounce from perch to perch and very often crouch on the perch and at the same time flap their wings vigorously. Their beak would have almost turned black by now. The cocks become very active and sometimes go through the vigorous flapping of wings routine. Cocks in breeding condition spend a lot of time singing and their beaks change to a pearly white.

Colony Breeding

Many aviculturists prefer the colony breeding system and whilst it may not be as selective as cage breeding, good quality birds could be produced if the aviculturist selects the breeding stock carefully. If size and colour is the criteria then all the birds in the colony should be selected with that in mind. The number of pairs in a breeding colony should be commensurate with the size of the aviary. By setting up more pairs in order to produce more youngsters, the problem of overcrowding is created which in turn causes stress. Birds that are under stress are more likely to contract a bacterial infection because of their lowered resistance. In fact, instead of producing more youngsters the breeder is more likely to finish up with less youngsters being bred. Birds which are inferior should not be selected for breeding. Improvement is gradual and may take several generations to achieve.

Courtship Behaviour

Not long after the birds are put together the cocks start courting and pairing up for the season. The courtship performance generally takes place on a perch or a horizontal branch. It consists of two phases. In the first phase the cock perches obliquely. The face and head feathers are fluffed while at the same time the breast and abdomen feathers are also fluffed making the purple breast patch look bigger. Showing these brilliant colours to the hen is not enough to attract her attention. The cock must "display" to the hen and this is done by first making a series of head movements in which the beak is wiped across the perch sometimes without touching it. This is followed by shaking his head to and fro

1 - A Red-headed Gouldian in courtship display.

1 - Cock Gouldians are in charge of nest building.

1 - WILSON MOORE

extremely rapidly in front of the hen. Suddenly the cock enters the second phase of his display. He adopts an upright stance on the perch and with his beak pointing downwards he starts bobbing up and down on the perch in a rigid stance as he sings his courtship song to the hen. This display is repeated several times during the courtship period. If the hen is receptive she will remain near him and will respond by twisting her tail towards him. If on the other hand she is unimpressed she will then fly away.

This is the time to put the nest boxes in place. The type I use is a 130mm (5in) cube with an opening of about one third of the box's height. I prefer this type of opening to a round hole entry. It makes inspection and monitoring of eggs and chicks a lot easier. Always provide at least fifty percent more boxes than pairs, in fact if a good supply is on hand two boxes to each pair will overcome all the nesting problems. Each nest has a preformed nest chamber of fine nesting material such as Couch, November grass or similar. Some pairs are poor nest builders whilst others build very elaborate nests finishing off with a canopy. Nesting material should be supplied in liberal quantities in lengths of about 100-150mm (4-5in) in wire baskets away from perches so as not to be fouled with droppings. Alternatively, it could be placed in a corner on the aviary floor where some birds seem to prefer it. Within minutes of the nest boxes being put in place the cock birds are peering inside from the top of the box without entering it. The hen which is never far from the cock may sometimes inspect the box soon after the cock. The cock carries all the nesting material and builds the nest while the hen watches. When the cock finishes building the hen enters the nest box and as egg laying time approaches they spend more time together in the nest box. Successful copulation takes place inside the nest box. Many a time a cock tries to mate on a perch without success. The hen often rejects him instantly.

Producing Eggs, Hatching and Rearing them.

Within ten to fifteen days, sometimes longer, depending at which stage of breeding condition they are in, the hens start laying. They produce one white egg every day, which is generally laid in the morning. Clutches vary in size from four to seven and sometimes more. On the third egg they invariably, although not

2 - DR ROB MARSHALL

always, start incubating. Some pairs do not start sitting in earnest until the last egg is laid. Incubation is shared during the day while at night the hen incubates on her own. When in breeding condition during the breeding season the cock and the hen develop a bare patch of skin on the abdomen. This brooding patch allows closer contact and better heat transfer to the eggs. On the fifth day of incubation fertile eggs become pinkish in colour, and if placed over a light source, blood veins are visible indicating that the embryo is developing. As the embryo grows the egg becomes chalky in colour and on the fifteenth or sixteenth day hatching usually commences. Discarded eggshells are eaten by the parents, although at odd times one might see half a shell on the floor underneath the nest box. The chicks are fed by both parents. The crop of a newly hatched chick extends to both sides of his neck, but only the right side is filled with food for the first few days. As the chick grows both sides are filled. Their begging calls for food are loud and can be heard several metres away. Newly hatched Gouldian chicks are bare skinned (no down) and of a light flesh colour. Their eyes open on the seventh day and the primary feathers break through the skin on the eleventh to twelfth day.

Soft food mixed with sprouted seed is supplied twice a day, morning and late afternoon and enough is given to meet their demands. As the chicks grow so does the amount of soft food and sprouted seed, and one must ensure at all times that the parents have as much as they require. All soft food containers are removed from the aviary before nightfall. This will ensure no stale soft food is fed to the chicks first thing in the morning.

Gouldians do not normally object to nest inspections, and I recommend that the chicks be checked at least once daily, assuming that the parents do not strongly object. I prefer to carry out nest inspections late in the afternoon. The inspection is necessary I feel, to check the condition of the chicks; that their crops are full and that their skin is smooth and shiny. Chicks' droppings tell many a story. Their droppings should be firm, black or yellow in part (depending on type of soft food supplied)

1 - WILSON MOORE

1 - Some Gouldians hardly build a nest, others make a dome over the eggs.
2 - Gouldian chicks 1-2 days old.

Page 22

and the remainder white.

Chicks fledge on the twenty-fourth to twenty-sixth day and they very rarely go back to their nest to roost, instead they huddle together on a branch or perch, often flanked by their parents. They become self sufficient twelve to fifteen days after fledging. At about this time the parents are beginning to prepare for their next brood so the chicks are removed and put into holding cages and remain there until the end of the breeding season. When the breeding season is over the nesting shelves are all boarded up as stated earlier, and all the youngsters are transferred to the aviaries to moult and colour up.

Keeping Breeding Records and Ringing Birds

One cannot have complete control over one's hobby unless records are kept. The keeping of records allows the breeder to know what is going on within his complex at any given time. Records become invaluable when selecting and pairing next season's breeding stock. Records give the breeder an instant report on what birds he has, how many were bred that year, how many died and other relative information which unless recorded is very hard to remember.

Birds are identified by being rung with either closed aluminium rings or split coloured plastic rings. Plastic rings are available in an assortment of colours and have the advantage of allowing easy identification without having to net the birds. The serious Gouldian breeder should consider using closed aluminium rings with the year the bird was hatched recorded on it. Chicks should be close rung between six and nine days old. At this stage the ball of the foot is large enough to keep the ring on.

Not all finch rings are the same size and unless the correct size is used problems could arise. If the ring is too large the bird can get caught on branches, or the ring can slip down the leg on to the ball of the foot cutting the blood circulation and the foot can be permanently damaged. If the fitted ring is under size then as the bird matures and the leg becomes thicker, the blood circulation is cut off and given time the leg will wither away. One can always write down how to ring birds, but the best way to learn is to ask someone who rings his own birds to give you a demonstration on how it is done.

Failure to Breed

Failure to breed is mostly due to incompatibility, assuming of course the birds are in breeding condition. A bird which is not one hundred percent healthy will not attain 'breeding condition'. Incompatibility is not a problem when colony breeding because birds will choose their own partners. If, on the other hand, one is cage breeding or putting one pair of birds in a small aviary then one has to watch closely for signs of incompatibility. The cock always shows his keenness to pair by displaying to the hen soon after being introduced.

If, some days after introduction the birds start showing signs of aggression by beak fencing, perching apart and showing complete disinterest in each other, then it is time to separate them and try them with other mates.

Using Bengalese as Foster Parents

Using Bengalese Finches as foster parents to rear Gouldian Finches is not a widely used method in Australia. It is, however, used on a commercial scale in some European countries and the

The Bengalese Finch

USA. The Bengalese Finch is in fact called upon to rear most of the finches one can think of. In Australia it is used by some small scale breeders. The foster rearing method is much more labour intensified and therefore much more demanding on the breeder. The reasons become more obvious later in this chapter. Some breeders who use Bengalese Finches to foster rear Gouldians claim that parasite cycles eg. the parasite air sac mite, can be broken because the Bengalese Finch does not harbour the air sac mite parasite and therefore it cannot be passed on to the Gouldian youngster.

The use of Bengalese Finches to foster rear Gouldian Finches is a contentious issue. However, the use of foster rearing to establish a new mutation remains well justified. Had the foster rearing method not been used the Australian White-breasted Yellow Gouldian mutation may not have become reasonably established to date. It is now being bred on a small scale in New South Wales, Queensland and Victoria and it is hoped that those breeding it will do well enough to establish it beyond doubt.

One must never give in to the temptation to over producing youngsters when using Bengalese Finches as foster parents. Sacrificing quality for quantity is a very short term gain. In the long term production of substandard birds is detrimental to both the breeder and aviculture generally.

The Japanese had a thriving export trade at one stage, supplying Europe and the USA with large numbers of Gouldians, until the quality of the birds started to suffer because the breeders were over producing them. At that point the trade started to decline and it is now believed to be non existent.

A fear that is often talked about when using the foster-rearing method is imprinting. It is fair to say that up until now and by using present breeding techniques, which will be discussed later, it has not proved to be a great problem. Gouldians reared by Bengalese have repeatedly proved that they can rear their own youngsters. What could prove to be a problem is the use of Bengalese Finches to foster rear Gouldian chicks belonging to Gouldian parents which are themselves incapable of rearing their own. If such traits are of a genetic nature and we pass them on by using the foster rearing method then we are creating a strain of Gouldian which is incapable of rearing its own young. Under normal conditions such a strain of Gouldian will not be propagated because firstly, the parents are incapable of rearing their own and secondly, birds that are known to have such traits are not selected to breed naturally.

Not all Bengalese Finches make good foster parents. Some are better than others. Therefore, when buying Bengalese for fostering try and get firstly, **cage-bred** birds (as opposed to aviary-bred birds), secondly and if possible, youngsters from parents which themselves have been successful as foster parents. It is also essential to get good quality birds. One should apply the same criteria when buying Bengalese as when buying Gouldians. All too often they are treated in an inferior manner because they are readily available and inexpensive to buy. If one is to treat fostering Bengalese in an inferior manner, then the end result surely has to be the same. The Gouldian breeder is fortunate in that the Bengalese needs are almost identical to those of the

1 - DR ROB MARSHALL

Bengalese Set Up

1 - Young Gouldians with their Bengalese foster mother.

Gouldian Finch and if the Bengalese Finch is treated the same way then it is living very well.

Their diet should be identical to the Gouldian including the austerity period. The Bengalese can be stimulated into breeding any time of the year by giving it the same nutritious diet as given to the Gouldian Finch. Some breeders fly their Bengalese Finches in large flights at the end of the breeding season. I have found that when put back into cages for breeding it takes them too long to settle down.

The Bengalese Finch stock has to be maintained and it becomes necessary to breed youngsters from time to time to supplement stock. This is done by transferring eggs from those Bengalese which have proved to be excellent foster parents to those which have been less successful. It is hoped that the young will inherit their parent's good rearing qualities. In my case the problem with youngsters arises when I try to sex them. There appears to be no obvious difference between cock and hen Bengalese. My method of sexing them is to spend time observing the youngsters. A cock can be identified by its courtship display. During the display it extends all its feathers while bouncing along the perch and singing a repetitious song. Birds that do not display are assumed to be hens. Sexed birds are rung, using the correct sized rings. Split plastic red numbered rings are used for cocks and split yellow numbered rings for hens. Later on when paired their sex will be confirmed by either an absence of eggs or an abundance of them at the rate of two a day.

As far as I am aware no specific studies of Gouldian Finches imprinting on Bengalese has ever been conducted. But as stated earlier, avicultural experience suggests that imprinting does not appear to be a serious problem in so far as the Gouldian Finch is concerned. It has been shown that Gouldian youngsters reared by Bengalese Finches are capable of rearing their own successfully when paired together. Having said that I do not think we should

1 - DR ROB MARSHALL

throw caution to the wind. Gouldian Finches bred under Bengalese should always be observed for "un-Gouldian" behaviour. With this in mind, I recommend that Bengalese Finches used for fostering should be housed on their own.

I use cages measuring 450mm (1ft 6in) long by 300mm (1ft) deep and 350mm (1ft 2in) high to house the Bengalese. These cages are made of 1 inch x 1/2 inch mesh using special clips and pliers to fix sides to roof and bottom. The front of the cage should have all the required openings to enable the cage to be serviced from the outside. Opening allowances should be made for a breeding box, seed and water container, soft food container and an opening for access into the cage for catching birds when required. A metal tray is made for the bottom of the cage. The purpose of this tray is to make cage cleaning easier. It slides in and out through a slot made in the front. Some breeders use a box type cage with a wire front. The advantage with the box type is that disease can not be transmitted from one cage to another. But the same effect could be achieved by placing wire cages 100mm (4in) apart. One great advantage with the wire cage is hygiene. At the end of the breeding season it is taken out of the room and completely immersed in a tub in a solution of water and disinfectant.

The door and nest box opening can be made of the same 1 inch x 1/2 inch mesh. The wire door of course, is made larger than the opening it is required to cover. The door is hinged while the nest box door is hooked onto the opening when the nest box is not in use. The cages are placed against a wall in rows of three or four high.

Fostering

1 - The basic cage to house Bengalese as foster parents.

For those who would like to try fostering under Bengalese it is a good idea to put three pairs of Bengalese to every pair of Gouldians. That way one is assured of having enough Bengalese in the same nesting cycle when the Gouldians start laying. There are two ways of handling Gouldian eggs. One is to wait for the Gouldians to lay the full clutch of eggs before they are transferred

1 - DR ROB MARSHALL

2 - DR ROB MARSHALL

*1 - The breeding cage complete with nest box and food and water receptacles.
2 - A bank of breeding cages.*

to the Bengalese. The other is to collect the eggs daily from the Gouldians, marking them with a felt tip pen and placing them in a dish with bran or seed. If the latter is adopted then the eggs must be turned daily, so that the yoke of the egg oes not come to rest on the shell, thereby reducing the hatchability rate. It goes without saying that when the Gouldian eggs are transferred to the Bengalese, the Bengalese's own eggs are removed. The reason is twofold, firstly it is unwise and inadvisable to rear mixed broods of different species, the Bengalese may neglect to rear the Gouldian chicks preferring their own; secondly expecting the Bengalese to incubate, hatch and rear two clutches of eggs is a tall order. Gouldian eggs must be marked with a felt tip pen so that in the event of a clutch of eggs being transferred to the Bengalese while they themselves are still laying, then the newly laid Bengalese eggs are easily identified and removed. Bengalese Finches are very tolerant of nest inspection and are very adaptable parents. For example, youngsters can be transferred from one nesting pair of Bengalese to another without problems, assuming the youngsters being moved are of the same age as the youngsters in the nest they are being moved to. The introduction of small nestlings into broods of larger youngsters is not generally successful because when they are competing with their nest mates for food, they may not receive enough to survive.

The feeding and rearing procedure is the same as that applied to Gouldian Finches which are rearing their own. The youngsters grow and develop at the same rate as they do if reared by Gouldians. They fledge at the same age and are fully independent at twelve to fifteen days. At this stage they are removed from their foster parents and put into holding cages with other juvenile Gouldians as described earlier.

Imprinting

As stated earlier avicultural experience suggests that imprinting of Gouldian youngsters on Bengalese foster parents does not appear to be a serious problem. It has been shown that Gouldian Finches reared by Bengalese foster parents are capable of rearing their own when paired together.

In 1987 at the Fourth National Convention venued at Gosford, NSW Professor Klaus Immelmann lectured on how Zebra Finches foster-reared under Bengalese imprinted on their foster parents. On reaching maturity these foster-reared Zebras behaved and acted as if they were Bengalese Finches. Photographic slides shown by Professor Klaus Immelmann clearly demonstrated that upon reaching maturity, cock Zebras, given the opportunity to court either a Zebra hen or Bengalese hen, almost invariably directed their displays to Bengalese hens, while matured Zebra hens sought the attention of Bengalese cocks.

Immelmann discovered that the imprinting process appears to be irreversible in the case of foster-reared Zebras. A foster-reared Zebra cock when paired with a Zebra hen would eventually breed if kept away from Bengalese Finches, but this breeding experience did not destroy their desire to breed with Bengalese hens, and given half a chance Zebra cocks showed they still preferred to court Bengalese hens to their own kind.

There is no evidence to suggest that such problems exist with Bengalese-reared Gouldians.

1 - A Yellow-headed cock Gouldian.
2 - Yellow-headed Cock.
3 - A hen Black-headed with yellow-tipped beak.
4 - A pair of Gouldians at the nest box.

1 - WILSON MOORE
2 - WILSON MOORE
3 - WILSON MOORE

1 - Red-headed cock bird looking out of nesting box.
2 - A cock Black-headed Gouldian peering at his hen inside the box.
3 - A cock Red-head with youngster - uncoloured and showing the blue phospherous nodules.

Page 30

Mutations and Colour Breeding

Head Colours in the Gouldian Finch

There are three basic head colours in the Gouldian. These are Black, Red and Yellow. Ideally the various head colours should not be indiscriminately bred together. By doing so a number of motley blackish red or blackish yellow headed birds are produced. This is especially prevalent in hen birds. When selecting for head colour breeding special attention should be paid to the hens to be bred with. Black-headed hens especially should be a rich deep velvety black with absolutely no signs of a red or yellow feather showing through.

The only reasons for crossing head colours should be to one, improve the quality of the finch itself. That is, if all the Yellow-headed birds in the aviary are of poor quality ie. too small or have poor fertility then they should be mated through your other head colours to rectify these deficiencies. Buying good quality Yellow-headeds may seem a better solution but remember that a lot of problems can be brought into your established stock by new arrivals so only bring them in when absolutely necessary and be sure to follow the quarantine measures etc discussed in another section of this book or disaster will most certainly follow. The second reason would be to breed a mutation in the three head colours. That is, if for example, all your Dilute-backed Gouldians are Black-headed, then to produce Red-headed Dilutes they have to be paired to Red-headed birds.

The Red-head is sex-linked dominant. The Black-head is sex-linked recessive. The Yellow-head is autosomal recessive.

A Red-headed Gouldian has a red-tipped beak. The Black-headed can have a red-tipped beak or a yellow-tipped beak and the Yellow-headed has a yellow-tipped beak.

The normal Black-headed Gouldian has a red-tipped beak. However, when a Gouldian inherits both the characteristics for black and yellow headedness the black will mask the yellow. That is to say, it is a Yellow-headed bird with a black head and not simply a Black-headed split to Yellow-headed. Therefore because it is Yellow-headed it has a yellow-tipped beak. A Black-headed Gouldian split to Yellow will have a red-tipped beak.

In the following table of matings and expectations a bird that is split to a colour is denoted by an oblique (/) that is, Red/Black means a Red-headed bird split to Black-headed. YTB means a yellow-tipped beak.

PARENTS	**PROGENY**	
Cock x Hen	% Male	% Female
Red x Red	50% Red	50% Red
Red x Black	50% Red/Black	50% Red
Red/Black x Red	25% Red 25% Red/Black	25% Red 25% Black
Red/Black x Black	25% Red/Black 25% Black	25% Red 25% Black
Red x Yellow	50% Red/Yellow	50% Red/Yellow
Red/Yellow x Red/Yellow	12.5% Red 25% Red/Yellow 12.5% Yellow	12.5% Red 25% Red/Yellow 12.5% Yellow
Red/Yellow x Yellow	25% Red/Yellow 25% Yellow	25% Red/Yellow 25% Yellow
Red/Yellow x Red	25% Red 25% Red/Yellow	25% Red 25% Red/Yellow
Red x Red/Yellow	25% Red 25% Red/Yellow	25% Red 25% Red/Yellow
Red/Black x Yellow	25% Red/Yellow 25% Red/Black/Yellow	25% Red/Yellow 25% Black/Yellow
Red/Black/Yellow x Black/Yellow	6.25% Red/Black 6.25% Black 12.5% Red/Black/Yellow 12.5% Black/Yellow 6.25% Yellow/Black 6.25% Black YTB	6.25% Red 6.25% Black 12.5% Red/Yellow 12.5% Black/Yellow 6.25% Yellow 6.25% Black YTB
Red/Yellow x Black/Yellow	12.5% Red/Black 25% Red/Black/Yellow 12.5% Yellow/Black	12.5% Red 25% Red/Yellow 12.5% Yellow
Red x Black YTB	50% Red/Black/Yellow	50% Red/Yellow

Red/Yellow x Black YTB	25% Red/Black/Yellow 25% Yellow/Black	25% Red/Yellow 25% Yellow
Red/Black/Yellow x Black YTB	12.5% Red/Black/Yellow 12.5% Black/Yellow 12.5% Yellow/Black 12.5% Black YTB	12.5% Red/Yellow 12.5% Black/Yellow 12.5% Yellow 12.5% Black YTB
Red/Black x Black YTB	25% Red/Black/Yellow 25% Black/Yellow	25% Red/Yellow 25% Black/Yellow
Red/Black x Black/Yellow	12.5% Red/Black 12.5% Black 12.5% Red/Black/Yellow 12.5% Black/Yellow	12.5% Red 12.5% Black 12.5% Red/Yellow 12.5% Black/Yellow
Red x Black/Yellow	25% Red/Black 25% Red/Black/Yellow	25% Red 25% Red/Yellow
Red/Black/Yellow x Black	12.5% Red/Black 12.5% Black 12.5% Red/Black/Yellow 12.5% Black/Yellow	12.5% Red 12.5% Black 12.5% Red/Yellow 12.5% Black/Yellow
Red/Yellow x Black	25% Red/Black 25% Red/Black/Yellow	25% Red 25% Red/Yellow
Red/Black/Yellow x Red/Yellow	6.25% Red 6.25% Red/Black 12.5% Red/Yellow 12.5% Red/Black/Yellow 6.25% Yellow 6.25% Yellow/Black	6.25% Red 6.25% Black 12.5% Red/Yellow 12.5% Black/Yellow 6.25% Yellow 6.25% Black YTB
Red/Black/Yellow x Yellow	12.5% Red/Yellow 12.5% Red/Black/Yellow 12.5% Yellow 12.5% Yellow/Black	12.5% Red/Yellow 12.5% Black/Yellow 12.5% Yellow 12.5% Black YTB
Red/Black x Red/Yellow	12.5% Red 12.5% Red/Black 12.5% Red/Yellow 12.5% Red/Black/Yellow	12.5% Red 12.5% Black 12.5% Red/Yellow 12.5% Black/Yellow
Red/Black/Yellow x Red	12.5% Red 12.5% Red/Black 12.5% Red/Yellow 12.5% Red/Black/Yellow	12.5% Red 12.5% Black 12.5% Red/Yellow 12.5% Black/Yellow

Black x Black	50% Black	50% Black
Black x Red	50% Red/Black	50% Black
Black x Yellow	50% Red/Black/Yellow	50% Black/Yellow
Black x Red/Yellow	25% Red/Black 25% Red/Black/Yellow	25% Black 25% Black/Yellow
Black/Yellow x Red	25% Red/Black 25% Red/Black/Yellow	25% Black 25% Black/Yellow
Black/Yellow x Red/Yellow	12.5% Red/Black 25% Red/Black/Yellow 12.5% Yellow/Black	12.5% Black 25% Black/Yellow 12.5% Black YTB
Black/Yellow x Black/Yellow	12.5% Black 25% Black/Yellow 12.5% Black YTB	12.5% Black 25% Black/Yellow 12.5% Black YTB
Black/Yellow x Yellow	25% Red/Black/Yellow 25% Yellow/Black	25% Black/Yellow 25% Black YTB
Black x Black/Yellow	25% Black 25% Black/Yellow	25% Black 25% Black/Yellow
Black YTB x Black	50% Black/Yellow	50% Black/Yellow
Black x Black YTB	50% Black/Yellow	50% Black/Yellow
Black YTB x Black/Yellow	25% Black/Yellow 25% Black YTB	25% Black/Yellow 25% Black YTB
Black/Yellow x Black YTB	25% Black/Yellow 25% Black YTB	25% Black/Yellow 25% Black YTB
Black YTB x Black YTB	50% Black YTB	50% Black YTB
Black YTB x Yellow	50% Yellow/Black	50% Black YTB

Black YTB x Red/Yellow	25% Red/Black/Yellow 25% Yellow/Black	25% Black/Yellow 25% Black YTB
Black YTB x Red	50% Red/Black/Yellow	50% Black/Yellow
Yellow x Yellow	50% Yellow	50% Yellow
Yellow x Black	50% Red/Black/Yellow	50% Red/Yellow
Yellow x Black/Yellow	25% Red/Black/Yellow 25% Yellow/Black	25% Red/Yellow 25% Yellow
Yellow/Black x Yellow	25% Yellow 25% Yellow/Black	25% Yellow 25% Black YTB
Yellow/Black x Black/Yellow	12.5% Red/Black/Yellow 12.5% Black/Yellow 12.5% Yellow/Black 12.5% Black YTB	12.5% Red/Yellow 12.5% Black/Yellow 12.5% Yellow 12.5% Black YTB
Yellow/Black x Black	25% Red/Black/Yellow 25% Black/Yellow	25% Red/Yellow 25% Black/Yellow
Yellow x Red	50% Red/Yellow	50% Red/Yellow
Yellow/Black x Red	25% Red/Yellow 25% Red/Black/Yellow	25% Red/Yellow 25% Black/Yellow
Yellow x Red/Yellow	25% Red/Yellow 25% Yellow	25% Red/Yellow 25% Yellow
Yellow/Black x Red/Yellow	12.5% Red/Yellow 12.5% Red/Black/Yellow 12.5% Yellow 12.5% Yellow/Black	12.5% Red/Yellow 12.5% Black/Yellow 12.5% Yellow 12.5% Black YTB
Yellow x Black YTB	50% Yellow/Black	50% Yellow
Yellow/Black x Black YTB	25% Yellow/Black 25% Black YTB	25% Yellow 25% Black YTB

Mutations and Colour Breeding

Some of the current Gouldian Finch mutations that are being developed in Australia are as follows:

The White-breasted

This mutation is identical to the normal bird except that the purple breast is replaced by pure white. The White-breasted Gouldian can occur in all three head colours. It is recessive in its mode of inheritance. (See table at the end of this chapter).

The Australian White-breasted Yellow

This very beautiful mutation is one of the most sought after in Australia at the moment. It is called the Australian White-breasted Yellow to distinguish it from the White-breasted European Dilute. The Australian mutation is recessive. Red and Yellow-headed birds in this mutation can be produced but the Black-headed appear as light creamy yellow heads not black. This also happens in the Dilute-back mutation though the grey is darker.

In the nest young birds can be distinguished from Normals because they have white nodules on the sides of the beak as opposed to the blue nodules of the Normal Gouldian. When they leave the nest, young birds show variegated markings on their backs and bodies. The heaviness of these green, grey and white markings vary in amount from bird to bird. As they mature the "most desirable" birds lose these markings and develop a pure yellow back. Others retain the markings though usually to a lesser extent. A breeder reports that one youngster left the nest almost pure white only to moult into a lovely clear yellow. So there is still much to be learnt about this mutation. Whether the variegated birds are a separate pied mutation to that of the birds with clear yellow backs is still being debated.

The Dilute-backed

This recessive mutation first appeared in Queensland around 1945 and has to date still failed to become readily available. Many aviaries held reasonable numbers of these birds at various times. Examples such as these and the loss of other mutations in the past indicate the real problems many breeders were having with their Gouldians. Losses of normals were no real problem in those days. Trapped birds made replacements easy to obtain. However, Dilutes and the other mutations were not obtainable in this fashion and so they died out or became scarce not necessarily because they were weak birds but more probably because of poor management techniques.

The black throat or bib of the Normal is a creamy bluish white in the Dilute giving the Red and Yellow-headed birds the look of wearing a bonnet. The back is a creamy lime green colour. This mutation cannot produce melanin so that the Black-headed bird does not exist as in the Normal. Here the Black-headed variety has a silver grey head.

In the nest dilute chicks have red eyes. However within a few days of their eyes opening, the eyes darken to that of the Normal. Their skin is pink and their feathers are creamy coloured. (See photograph).

Lilac-breasted

This mutation only differs from the Normal in breast colour.

It first appeared in the United Kingdom through breeding White-breasted and split White-breasted Gouldians. In the beginning the lilac appeared as small patches on the White-breast and this was gradually improved. This is very interesting because in Australia these lilac patches are appearing on the breasts of some of our White-breasted mutations. One breeder here reports that a cock Red-headed White-breasted Yellow, when young showed these lilac patches and at the age of two years was completely lilac. This bird still showed the white base feathers beneath the lilac front. This mutation is apparently recessive to the Normal but dominant to the White-breasted. It can clearly be seen in the photograph of the Blue-backed cock.

The Lilac-breasted mutation should be treated with caution because it can easily spread through all your birds and pop up where it is unwanted. Purple breasted birds are the most dangerous because they can carry the lilac factor without visually showing it. The simplest way to eradicate the lilac factor from your birds is to breed the White-breasted mutations. Select those birds with pure white breasts because lilac is dominant to the white breast and if they do not show lilac then they are not carrying it. If there is the slightest speck of lilac on the breast then it is carrying lilac. The lilac will increase over one to two years to ultimately cover the breast.

The Blue-backed Gouldian

All the green in this bird is replaced by blue. The abdomen is creamy yellow to white. It can easily be distinguished from Dilute Blues because the Dilutes cannot produce melanin and they therefore lose the black bib and pencil line around the face that the Blue-back retains. Also black-headed Blue-backs can be produced. Like all the Blue mutations this is recessive and can occur in all three breast colours (purple, lilac and white). In all the Blue mutations so far the red or yellow beak-tip colours have been lost. In the nest Blue chicks have normal coloured eyes but their skins appear as a smokey, blue-grey haze.

The Sea-green

This is a very recent mutation to have been bred in Australia. Not a lot is known about it at present. A photograph of a Black-headed Sea-green hen shows that it is certainly different in colour to the other blue mutations.

The Yellow-backed Gouldian

Overseas this bird is often referred to as the European Dilute. This will confuse many Australian Gouldian breeders because it is not the same as the recessive Dilute-backed discussed earlier. So here we will refer to this mutation as the Yellow-back.

The genetics for this mutation is quite complicated and has not been totally worked out and confirmed at this point in time. Very basically it is a co-dominant sex-linked mutation. At this stage it would be more beneficial to the reader to write about some of things that happen with this mutation rather than why they happen.

All hens are single factor. No double factor Yellow-backed hens can be produced. The cock birds however can be single factor or double factor birds. There can only be one phenotype (physical appearance) in the double factor cock Yellow-back, so we will consider this bird first. This bird looks the same as the Yellow-backed hen in the photographs but has the usual brighter purple chest of the cock Gouldian. Overseas this bird is referred to as a European Yellow. This again is confusing because it sounds like a separate mutation and you cannot get a pair of European Yellows because only the cock bird can be a double factor. So here we shall refer to it as a double factor Yellow-back. Double factor Yellow-backed cocks occur in both purple and white-breasted forms.

The single factor Yellow-backed cock does not resemble a Yellow-back at all. From the photograph it can be seen that it looks like a diluted version of a Normal Gouldian. This is another example of where a name can cause much confusion. In America and Europe it is not referred to as a single factor Yellow-backed cock but as a Dilute. So when they refer to mating a Dilute to a Yellow-back this is not describing the crossing of two different mutations as many people could not be blamed for believing but it is simply mating a single factor Yellow-backed cock to a single factor Yellow-backed hen. This single factor cock can be distinguished quite easily from the Normal Gouldian cock. Not simply because the green on the back is lighter or because the blue on the neck and rump is a softer shade but the single factor bird does not show the black markings of the Normal. The black bib, the black face pencil line, the black flights and the black tail feathers are all replaced by a fawny grey.

So far we have been talking about the Normal purple-breasted Yellow-back in single and double factor form. When the White-breasted Gouldian is crossed with the Yellow-back more changes take place. When White-breasted Yellow-backs are produced their entire body goes yellow. These birds look very much like the recessive Australian White-breasted Yellows. The hens are much more yellow on the back than the cocks. The cocks show the dilute effects typical of the single factor Yellow-backed cock. He has a soft green wash through his back and the bib and neck markings are a grey-blue. (See photographs).

When comparing the White-breasted and purple-breasted Yellow-backs it is hard to believe that differences have only been brought about by a change in breast colour. Overseas White-breasted Yellow-backs are referred to as Yellow-bodied Gouldians. We will now look at the effect the blue gene has on the Yellow-backed Gouldian. When the Blue-backed Gouldian is bred through the Yellow-back the young produced in the first generation will include Yellow-backed hens split Blue, Normal hens split Blue, single factor Yellow-backed cocks split Blue and Normal cocks split Blue. It is in the second generation that we can expect to produce another mutation from the blue and yellow-backed genes. Here we find that the blue series hens produced are either Blue or single factor Silver and the cocks produced are single factor Blue Yellow-backs (called Pastel Blue in America and Light Blue in Europe) and double factor Blue Yellow-backs called Silvers. It should be emphasised here that we are discussing purple-breasted Blues and Silvers. The Pastel or Light Blue or Blue Dilute Gouldian cock is equivalent to a single factor purple-breasted Silver.

The Pastel or single factor Blue Yellow-backed cock is a beautiful bird of soft powdery blue colouring. (See photographs).

When the White-breasted mutation is put through these birds, White-breasted Blue-backed hens and White-breasted Silver hens can be produced but in the cocks White-breasted Pastel Blues (or White-breasted Blue single factor Yellow-backs) cannot be produced. Instead this bird is a White-breasted Silver.

In a nutshell then, hens can only be purple or White-breasted single factor Silvers and cocks can only be double factor purple or White-breasted Silvers, single factor White-breasted Silvers or purple-breasted Pastel Blues (the equivalent of a purple-breasted single factor Silver).

In the Yellow-backs and their combinations only the Red and Yellow heads show colour. The Black-headed birds vary from a silver-grey to a creamy-white. So the closest we are going to get to a black-eyed White Gouldian at the moment is the Black-headed White-breasted Silver. (See photograph of a young one).

It should be mentioned here that when breeding from certain double factor combinations a certain percentage of chicks produced will die in the nest. This is due to a lethal factor. It is unwise therefore to breed double factor cocks with single factor hens. Double factor cocks should be bred with Normals or Blues to produce all single factor birds.

In the nest Yellow-backed chicks at first have lighter eyes than the Normal but these darken again around seven days after opening. Their skin is more of a yellow orange colour, very much like a jaundice effect.

Silver chicks eyes also start off lighter but darken to that of the Normal. Their skin is a hazey silver-blue colour.

Briefly then, we have discussed the following mutations all steming from the Yellow-backed Gouldian. The European Dilute (single factor Yellow-backed cock), the European Yellow (double factor purple-breasted Yellow-backed cock), the Pastel Blue (the blue single factor Yellow-backed cock) and the Silver.

There is still a long way to go with mutations of Gouldian Finches in Australia. Blues and Sea-greens still have to be crossed to the recessive Australian White-breasted Yellows and the Dilute-backs to name a few.

Further updates on these and new mutations in Australia will be appearing in Australian Birdkeeper magazine as more information and breeding results can be realised.

As more and more mutations appear it is advisable that the names given to them are not confusing and that they be accepted world-wide otherwise no one will be quite sure what bird is being bought, sold or described.

Recessive Inheritance Table

In the following table just substitute the letter 'c' for the recessive mutation colour. Examples of recessive mutations are Dilute-backed, White-breasted, Blue and the Australian White-breasted Yellow.

NN = A normal bird
cc = A recessive coloured bird
Nc = A normal split to a recessive colour

> NN x NN = 100% NN
>
> NN x cc = 100% Nc
>
> Nc x cc = 50% Nc and 50% cc
>
> NC x Nc = 50% Nc and 25% NN and 25% cc
>
> Nc x NN = 50% Nc and 50% NN
>
> cc x cc = 100% cc

To conclude this chapter, not enough importance can be placed upon the breeding of Normals. With all the mutations that are present now and those that will be produced in the future we must all endeavour not to forget the Normal bird. Overseas breeders cannot import Normal Gouldians from Australia and here in their native country the wild populations are declining. The fate of these birds could now rest in the hands of aviculturists. Mutations have their place but not at the expense of the Normal bird. It could well be that in the future the Normal Gouldian will be more sought after than any mutation but it should be before that situation arises that we ensure the safety of these really magnificent finches.

1 - Australian White-breasted Yellow.
2 - Yellow-headed Australian White-breasted Yellow.
3 - Two juvenile White-breasted Yellows.
4 - A pair of Australian White-breasted Yellows. (Red-headed hen and Yellow-headed cock.

Page 42

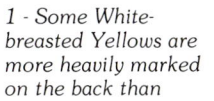

1 - Some White-breasted Yellows are more heavily marked on the back than others.
2 - This Red-headed White-breasted Yellow is much clearer on the back.
3 - A cock Black-headed Dilute-backed Gouldian.
4 - Adult White-breasted Yellow and youngster.

1 - WILSON MOORE
2 - GREG WIGHTMAN
3 - GREG WIGHTMAN
4 - GREG WIGHTMAN

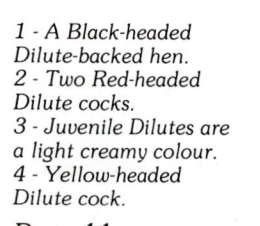

1 - A Black-headed Dilute-backed hen.
2 - Two Red-headed Dilute cocks.
3 - Juvenile Dilutes are a light creamy colour.
4 - Yellow-headed Dilute cock.

Page 44

1 - DR ROB MARSHALL

4 - DR ROB MARSHALL

3 - WILSON MOORE

2 - DR ROB MARSHALL

1 - This mutation is similar to the normal except for the breast colour.
2 - A cock Red-headed White-breasted Gouldian.
3 - Yellow-headed White-breasted cock.
4 - A Black-headed White-breasted hen and a Yellow-headed Australian White-breasted Yellow cock.

Page 45

1 - Back view of a Yellow-backed hen.
2 - Yellow-backs cannot produce melanin therefore have no black throats.
3 - A Yellow-backed hen. (European Dilute).
4 - A Yellow-backed hen. The double factor Yellow-backed cock is similar but has a brighter purple chest.

Page 46

1 - A White-breasted Yellow-backed cock just completing his moult.
2 - A White-breasted Yellow-backed hen. (These are called Yellow-bodied overseas).
3 - The White-breasted Yellow-backed hen is not unlike the White-breasted Australian Yellow.
4 - The back of a White-breasted Yellow-backed cock showing the dilution effect.

Page 47

1 - A Black-headed Sea-green hen.
2 - Green and Yellow are replaced by Blue and White in the Blue-backed Gouldian.
3 - A Blue-backed hen Gouldian. Note there is no coloured tip to the beak.
4 - A Yellow-headed Lilac-breasted Gouldian cock.

Page 48

1 - A single factor Yellow-backed cock (left) is a "diluted" version of the Normal.
2 - A Dilute or single factor Yellow-backed cock looks nothing like his hen.
3 - Single factor Yellow-backed cocks show no black markings unlike the Normal.

Page 49

1 - Pastels are beautiful shades of powdery blue, only cocks show this colouring.
2 - Pastel Blues show no black markings and never have white breasts.
3 - A Pastel Blue or Blue single factor Yellow-backed cock.
4 - Yellow-headed Silver cock (purple-breasted cocks are double factor Yellow-backs).

Page 50

1 - WILSON MOORE

2 - WILSON MOORE

3 - WILSON MOORE

*1 - A young Black-headed White-breasted Silver cock. (Approaching the White Gouldian).
2 - Purple-breasted Silver cock.
3 - Purple-breasted Silver hen.*

1 - WILSON MOORE
3 - WILSON MOORE
2 - WILSON MOORE

1 - A Yellow-headed, lilac over White-breasted Blue-backed Gouldian cock.
2 - This bird would be even more striking with a white rather than lilac breast.
3 - There is not a hint of yellow or green on a good Blue-backed Gouldian.

1 - *A rich strong blue like this is desirable in any blue bird mutation.*
2 - *A Yellow-headed Lilac over White-breasted Blue-backed Gouldian cock.*

1 - This Black-headed hen has hatched and is rearing ten babies.
2 - Normal Gouldian chicks. Notice the dark skin markings (especially on the head) and the dark feathers.
3 - Normal Gouldian chicks.
4 - A nest of Dilute-backed chicks. Their skin lacks the dark markings of the Normals and their feathers are a lighter fawn colour. Though this photo doesn't show it their eyes are red at this stage.

Page 54

The Health of the Gouldian Finch

A strong natural constitution is a prerequisite for the continuing good health of the Gouldian Finch. The development of this natural resistance to disease is a good reflection of proper avicultural practice.

It is not easy to develop a "strong" strain of Gouldian Finches because over the years the needs of this beautiful bird have been misunderstood. The Gouldian has been unfairly tagged as a bird which is difficult to breed because of its apparent susceptibility to disease.

Many of the illnesses of Gouldians have not been completely understood until recent years. In previous times the illnesses were treated empirically and often medications were and are still misused. Some Gouldian breeders medicate continuously for problems which may no longer be present. Such inappropriate use of medications serves only to inhibit a strong natural resistance in the Gouldian aviary, thereby perpetuating the myth that this bird is susceptible to disease.

Gouldians which have been fed and housed properly are prolific and healthy breeders.

Proper nutrition plays a very important part in maintaining the health of the Gouldian Finch. The Gouldian Finch has a particularly high need for protein during the breeding season and sub-optimal levels during this period may cause poor parenting and nestling illness. Juveniles on a low protein diet are especially prone to illness during their first moult. Infertility and poor breeding results due to vitamin deficiencies may occur on a diet consisting of seed alone. Poor nutrition decreases the natural resistance of the bird to illness. Gouldians may well thrive on an all seed diet in the "austere" or off-season when the

1 - DR ROB MARSHALL

2 - WILSON MOORE

1 - Clean and healthy Gouldians.
2 - It is not easy to develop a strong robust strain of Gouldian.

Page 56

nutritional needs are least and other physiological stresses are low. However, illness will eventually occur in the more stressful breeding or moulting seasons if the birds are not fed or not accustomed to a soft food diet high in protein and balanced in vitamins and minerals.

A healthy Gouldian with a good resistance can tolerate most stresses if they occur singularly, however, even a bird which has an extremely hardy constitution will succumb to illness when more than one stress occurs at the same time. A stress free environment lowers the opportunity for illness to occur by preventing the overlapping of these stresses. (Refer to the chapter on aviary functions and design.)

Nearly all diseases that occur in the Gouldian aviary can be related to stress, a "carrier" bird or a bird with a poor constitution.

Either "stress", the "carrier" bird or genetic weakness is the origin of all disease in the aviary. "Stress" is anything which upsets the birds normal routine. The "stress response" is the rapid release of adrenalin and acts as a protective mechanism for escape from predators in the wild. In captive birds, the stress response is too long lived and renders the bird susceptible to illness. A large part of disease control in the Gouldian aviary is to limit stress.

Stress can be either physical or psychological. Some examples that can cause Gouldians stress include overcrowding, poor nutrition, sudden change in feeding routine, dirty or decaying foods, dirty water, moist aviary, dirty floors, lack of adequate sunshine, noise, sudden temperature variation and temperature extremes, incompatible individuals, age groups or species, a new aviary, transporting birds, breeding, moulting, most medications have a stressful effect on the Gouldian, predators such as Butcher Birds, Currawongs, snakes, Kookaburras, rodents, improper perch or breeding box placement. Perches or food placed too low to the ground (a Gouldian in the wild will not land on the ground for water unless there is absolutely no danger. They would rather fly three hours to a safe water hole. It is a matter of survival. This behaviour has carried over to the aviary situation).

Disease is always associated with "stress" in the Gouldian Finch and control of illness relies on limiting both the physical and psychological stressful situations.

The "carrier" bird is one which appears healthy but is capable of infecting other birds (i.e. it carries a disease) and itself may become ill or die under times of stress. A "carrier" bird can only be detected by special tests performed by an avian veterinarian. There is no practical and cost effective way for a Gouldian breeder to detect "carrier" birds, however by limiting stress and "quarantining" the "carrier" bird when it arrives at the Gouldian aviary , then the danger of the "carrier" bird is considerably lessened. Several diseases of Gouldians, notably Cochlosomasis, Coccidiosis, Klebsiella, many other bacterial infections and Chlamydiosis can be transmitted by the "carrier" bird.

"Stress" will cause a "carrier" bird to become ill or die.

The final part of disease origins in the Gouldian aviary is the weakling bird. Such a bird is genetically weak and is unable to withstand even a low grade infection. Illness appears at an early age and usually occurs in a slowly developing nestling. It is important not to "save" these birds with the use of medication or hand-rearing, because they are a source of contamination to the whole flock. These are the birds most likely to become "carriers" if they survive past the first juvenile moult. The breeding programme must eliminate breeding pairs which produce "weaklings".

Often a change of partners will halt the production of weakling birds. Sometimes however it is necessary to introduce "outside" blood to strengthen your family of Gouldians.

Good hygiene lowers the number of potential germs in the aviary.

Even the most hardy Gouldians will become ill if the aviary environment is highly contaminated with pathogens. Bacteria and fungi infections of the Gouldian Finch are commonly associated with poor nutrition, together with unhygienic conditions. Poor quality seed (less than 80% sprouting rate), dusty old seed, decomposing vegetable and fruit matter, an aviary floor which is left dirty or left uncleaned, water which is not changed and cleaned daily, moisture in the aviary which may initiate mould and fermentation, exposure to the elements heat, cold, rain and wind all affect the overall health and vitality of the Gouldian Finch.

Long term bacterial disease control of the water with Aviclens$^{(T)}$ or other disinfectants is a worthy short term control measure but should not be used as a substitute for proper hygienic principles.

Health Aspects of the Newly Acquired Gouldian Finch

When new birds are introduced to an established Gouldian aviary there is always a danger of the introduction of undesirable genes or infectious disease agents. The best way of controlling disease in a "closed" aviary is to prevent infected birds from entering the breeding population, however it is not always possible to detect such birds without the help of an avian veterinarian. That said, there is a very good chance of identifying those potentially dangerous Gouldians if certain guidelines are

1 - The quarantine facility should be away from the breeding aviaries.

1 - DR ROB MARSHALL

followed. Only good stock from known reputable sources (i.e. Gouldian breeders and specialist bird shops rather than the local pet shop) should be purchased. However even then a bird in the incubation stage of disease may appear healthy. Therefore, regardless of the source, all newly acquired Gouldians should be kept in isolation (i.e. quarantine for at least 30 days). A properly managed quarantine system will exclude the most important diseases and also reduce the risk of other diseases. However, it must always be remembered that quarantine can never always be 100% effective.

The quarantine facility should be away from the breeding aviary.

There are several quarantine and isolation considerations to discuss. As previously mentioned it is important to obtain only healthy birds from a "clean" source. When selecting Gouldian Finches one must consider which groupings of birds are at lowest risk of contracting disease. Gouldians must be completely through the first juvenile moult before being considered. Unfortunately, Gouldian Finches are very susceptible to illness under poor management conditions during this first juvenile moult. The first moult is a considerable energy and protein drain on the body mechanisms of the Gouldian and it is at this time that many illnesses occur. A three week period after the completion of this moult renders the Gouldian resistant to most illnesses and prepares the Gouldian for a successful trouble free change of aviary. It is necessary to identify the completion of the moult by ensuring that all primary flight and tail feathers are complete.

A physical examination of every Gouldian Finch is necessary before purchase.

All birds have the ability to hide signs of illness and this is thought to be a protective mechanism in the wild. "Eye-ball" examination of a Gouldian through the wire of an aviary or cage will not give a clear indication of the health of the individual. The physical examination of the breast muscle for signs of "going

1 - The breast should be examined for signs of going light.

1 - DR ROB MARSHALL

Page 59

light" (i.e. prominent keel), the eyes for signs of discharge and swelling, the vent for signs of pasting, the feathers for the stage of moult and condition, and by listening carefully to the breathing of the new Gouldian gives a much better indication as to the health and vitality of the new bird. Gouldians with abnormalities of any kind should not be purchased.

In short, purchase a Gouldian Finch which has completed its first juvenile moult and which has passed a physical health examination.

The Gouldian which has completed the first juvenile moult successfully is the preferred new Gouldian. Older mature Gouldians are less desirable unless they are proven breeders and eat a varied diet. It is difficult to teach older birds new feeding habits and the success with Gouldian breeding relies heavily on proper nutrition "Old" hens may carry ovary infections which are impossible to detect and represent a considerable danger to the resident breeding population.

The final selection of the new healthy Gouldian depends on its physical attributes.

Larger, robust birds reflect good nutrition and aviary

1 - Wing examination will show if the moult is complete. The end primary flights are last to moult.
2 - An abnormal beak is an indication of disease.

management and are considered positively as a source of desirable new genes for the resident flock. Gouldians from highly inbred flocks are not recommended for these birds are both poor specimens physically and also more likely to succumb to illness.

The life of the Gouldian for two weeks after purchase is an extremely stressful psychological experience and all efforts must be made to minimise the physical hardships these new birds must endure.

Careful transport and clean handling is recommended after the purchase. The transport cage should be kept covered and cleaned before use. The holding isolation cage at home should be ready for use before the purchase of the birds. The design of this quarantine facility is such so as to give the new Gouldian complete confidence in its new home. A "hide" area is an important part of the quarantine cage, as are feeding and water containers which are well elevated. The aim of the isolation exercise is to minimise stress to the new bird whilst it adjusts to its new home. As well, it allows time for any incubating illness to surface without endangering the health of the entire resident flock (careful observation of the new birds is essential to detect any early signs of illness). Any medications should be with-held for the first two weeks of quarantine unless early signs of illness are detected. Ideally dropping samples of the new birds should be submitted to an avian veterinarian for analysis. The health status of the new residents is then known and appropriate measures can be taken to maintain their health whilst in quarantine. An informed treatment programme can then be given without any question of using unnecessary medication at an inappropriate time.

In situations where an avian veterinarian is not required the following protocol should be followed for all new birds during their stay in the quarantine facility.

Firstly the birds should be carefully observed daily from a distance during their stay in quarantine. Any birds manifesting the typical sick Gouldian look (fluffed up with two feet on the ground or perch) or showing abnormal droppings should be moved to a hospital "hot box" for further observation, analysis and treatment. The hospital cage should have paper on the floor so that the droppings can be monitored. The character of abnormal droppings may alert the fancier to a particular problem. It is important not to medicate Gouldians during the first two "stressful" weeks of quarantine unless there is illness and then only those individuals which are unwell are treated and done so in a hospital box. The birds in quarantine should not be disturbed during the first two weeks. Water and food replenishment should be done without entering the cage.

After the first two weeks of acclimatization in quarantine a quick health analysis is performed. This is done by placing paper beneath the perches for a day and observing the nature of the droppings and a preventative health programme can be initiated. At this time all new Gouldians should be treated for air sac mite and tapeworms prior to entering the main aviary. Air sac mite is best treated using Ivermectin via the "spot-on" technique whilst the tapeworm is treated with Droncit (via soft food or water). Other medication, especially antibiotics should not be given to Gouldians unless there is a bacterial infection.

At the end of the thirty days of quarantine the new Gouldians should be active and alert, happy with their new home and showing no signs of illness (note especially the droppings). The healthy birds are then moved to the aviary in the morning and observed for signs of aggression. Birds with untidy head feathers have been brutalized by the resident flock and should be moved to an empty section of the aviary. Any birds which are not 100% healthy should stay in quarantine until they are well.

The life and needs of the Gouldian Finch vary according to the seasons; breeding season, the moulting season and the off season all have specific requirements and illness may occur if these needs are not adequately met. The disease and preventative health programmes of the Gouldian Finch are best discussed according to the season in which they most commonly occur.

The "breeding season is a physically demanding time for both the adult and nestling Gouldian alike.

The adult Gouldian Finch must endure tremendous physical effort during the "breeding" season activities of courtship, nesting, laying eggs and the feeding of a large clutch of nestlings. The baby Gouldian as well expends tremendous amounts of resources in its development from the hatched embryo to the fully fledged juvenile.

Nutrition plays a most important part in the health of the Gouldian Finch during the breeding season.

Many of the diseases of the breeding season are directly or indirectly related to a deficient diet in the Gouldian Finch breeding aviary. The proper nutrition of the Gouldian during the breeding season involves not only the content of the diet but also the cleanliness of both the food and water.

It is known that the Gouldian Finch requires high levels of protein and energy to sustain its activities of the breeding season. These requirements can be met in many different forms depending upon the individual aviculturist's preferences. Sprouted seeds may be preferred over seeding grasses for the energy and vitamin requirements of the breeding season, simply because of the irregular availability of the seeding grasses. Whatever your preference as an aviculturist, it is necessary first of all, to understand the nutritional value of the food stuffs that are fed to your Gouldians.

The seed part of the Gouldians diet provides the minimal requirements necessary for survival. The Gouldian Finch in the wild has a considerably more varied diet than seed alone, consisting also of grasses, insects, and dirt. The breeding season of the Gouldian is stimulated by the "wet" season rains of northern Australia which provide the finch with a plentiful supply of seeding grasses and insect life. The seeding grasses yield the high energy carbohydrates, medium levels of protein and a good supply of both fat and water soluble vitamins. The insects provide the extra high quality protein. The abundance of this highly nutritious food has allowed the finch to develop into a prolific breeder.

Predators are easily attracted to the brilliant hues of this magnificent finch and the strong evolutionary forces have necessitated it to be a prolific breeder. The Gouldian Finch has evolved dependent upon the presence of seeding grasses and insects. In the aviary situation the same high levels of nutrition must be provided if the Gouldian is to breed successfully. This does not necessarily mean that insects or seeding grasses must be fed. There are many alternatives which will satisfy the needs of the Gouldian during the breeding season. One such breeding season diet has been documented in this book.

A high level of protein (e.g. insects, worms or hard boiled egg) and a high energy/vitamin food (e.g. seeding grasses, sprouted or soaked seed) as well as minerals (grit, charcoal, soil etc.) is necessary for the Gouldian to breed successfully.

The Causes of Disease in the Gouldian Finch

The management procedures must be carefully examined when illnesses occur within the Gouldian aviary.

It has already been noted that most diseases occur during the critical stress periods of moulting, breeding, fledgling and recaging. This occurs because there has been an overlapping of stress to the finch. It is necessary to identify the nature of problem to rectify the source of overlapping stress and then to treat the illness with the appropriate medication. Only then will the disease or illness be totally cured. If the disease is to be cured (rather than temporarily controlled with the use of medications) it is then necessary for the breeder to identify the problem area. He/she would then be able to treat the disease with the appropriate medication and prevent its recurrence by rectifying the source of the overlapping stress.

The following checklist for the aviculturist will help identify the source of the overlapping stress.

The problem in the aviary may be associated with:-
(i) Water hygiene
(ii) Food hygiene (seed, softfood, greens)
(iii) Aviary hygiene
(iv) Nutrition
(v) Quarantine procedure
(vi) Insect, rodent, predator control
(vii) Medications
(viii) Temperature control
(iv) Foster parents
(x) The carrier bird
(xi) Overcrowding

Water Hygiene

Contaminated water is a common cause of bacterial septicaemias in the adult Gouldian.

The water must be fresh daily and the water containers scrubbed clean and disinfected (Chlorhexidine/Halamid etc.) at least once a week. Water from a hose carries potentially harmful bacteria (Pseudomonas). Water collected from a running tap without a rubber/plastic attachment is preferred.

Those birds which survive the infection may become "carriers" of the disease. The infection commonly localises in the ovary of such birds causing infertility, dead in shell, dying nestlings (2-3 days old). Sudden death in the fledglings and young adults during the juvenile moult may also occur with this bacterial infection. An outbreak of bacterial infection related to contaminated water is controlled by a short course of the appropriate antibiotic and the disinfection of the aviary and water containers.

The long term prevention of this disease requires continuing

1 - The first sign of disease in 3-5 day old nestlings is red skin (dehydration) and retarded growth. Appropriate medication at this time will save this nest.

good water hygiene and the elimination of any ornamental bird baths, weather proofing the aviary from prevailing winds and rain and cementing over any areas of dirt floor and collecting water from the tap rather than from a hose.

Symptoms of Disease Related to Poor Water Hygiene

Symptoms of weight loss and diarrhea associated with the following:-
1. Sudden adult deaths during breeding season.
2. Infertility
3. Dead in shell
4. Dying 3 day old babies
5. Illness during moult and at fledgling
6. Recurring illness after the use of the appropriate antibiotics.

Food Hygiene

The Gouldian Finch cannot tolerate excessive levels of bacteria or fungus in the diet.

Bread crumbs (biscuits etc.) are prone to fungal contamination (eg. blue mould on old bread) and an imperfect sprouting technique can cause heavy bacterial and yeast infections in the Gouldian Finch. The proper preparation of the soft food mix is imperative to the health of the breeding Gouldian Finch and its offspring. The uneaten remnants of the soft food mix, greens and other fresh foodstuff additives must be removed from the aviary within six hours to prevent the dangers of bacterial fermentation and potential disease caused by this "rotting" food.

Symptoms of Disease Related to Poor Food Hygiene

Non specific signs of illness with watery droppings associated with the following:-
1. Sudden death of all ages and either sex at any time of the year.
2. Humid weather and the "spoilage" of soft food or greens in the aviary.
3. A new batch of seed.
4. Feeding sprouts with an offensive odour.

Sprouting Hygiene

The critical parts of good sprouting technique include the use of clean, disease free seed (i.e. seed free of dust, bacteria and fungus); the use of glass sprouting containers scrubbed clean and disinfected after each use with a broad spectrum "safe to drink" disinfectant (e.g. Halamid or Aviclens by Vetafarm). Chlorhexidine (Aviclens) or other appropriate disinfectants used in the sprouting process is a good idea but they will not control disease if the seed used for sprouting is heavily contaminated with bacteria or fungus. The water must be from a fresh source. Use water from the tap rather than from a hose.

Sprouting Procedure

For a long time aviculturists have used sprouted seed to supplement the diet of Gouldians. The benefits of sprouted seed cannot be disputed, however, a perfect technique is necessary to eliminate the potential problems associated with the sprouting process.

The Benefits

Sprouted seed provides the feeding adult with all the benefits of a seed diet together with a highly palatable source of easily digested energy and protein for the growing nestling.

For this reason the feeding process is less strenuous on the breeding pair and there is less likelihood of the "poor parent syndrome". Babies fed a mixed sprouted seed diet readily accept a varied balanced diet as fledglings. Sprouted seed is not necessary outside the breeding season.

The Equipment

Glass and stainless steel is preferred to plastic for the soaking and sprouting containers.

The porous nature of plastic prevents the sterilisation of a container contaminated by bacteria or other disease forming germs. Glass and stainless steel are easily sterilised in boiling water or with appropriate disinfectants. Plastic can be used successfully until infected, however thereafter it will be impossible to control sprouting related diseases in the aviary.

The Seed

The seed, above all else, is the most important part of the sprouting process. The seed type, quality and cleanliness are all equally important.

Seed Type

A variety of seed types is recommended so that the nestlings will accept a varied diet as fledglings and adults.

The main seeds used for sprouting are the "oil" seeds (high energy and high protein) although often the "starch" seeds (high energy and lower protein) are best given before hatching and when the young are fully feathered. The high energy and high protein seeds such as rape and lettuce, are easy to sprout and highly palatable. The "starch" seeds such as the millets, canary and wheat should be given for variety and for the correct protein balance. Some seeds such as niger seed are almost impossible to sprout without special laboratory techniques.

Seed Quality

An 80% and above sprouting rate reflects a seed of good quality.

There is no nutritional value in a seed (except niger) which does not readily sprout.

Seed Cleanliness

Most seed merchants realise the value of clean seed for the prevention of disease.

Dusty and unclean seed is more likely to be contaminated with bacteria and fungus than a seed that has been cleaned. Seed to be used for sprouting must be clean.

Seed grown by irrigation is sometimes contaminated by fungus. Fungus infections are a common cause of illness and breeding failure. The millets are the grains most commonly affected. Any suspect grains should be cultured and titrated in order to detect the levels of contamination with fungus and bacteria or be left in direct sunlight for several hours before being used for sprouting.

The Water

Water hygiene is a necessary part of a successful sprouting technique. Water collected from a hose may carry potential disease forming bacteria (e.g. Pseudomonas) and should not be used. It is best to use water from a tap without plastic fittings.

The Process

The correct sprouting process must be used in order to minimise the potential problems associated with the technique.

1. Soak seed for twelve hours in a sterilised container (preferably glass or stainless steel) using clean seed.

2. After 12 hours strain seed and wash repeatedly until the water is clean. Abort the process if the seed has an offensive odour at this time. The seed should have a sweet smell.

3. After the cleansing and straining, leave strained seed in a warm place, repeating the above (2.) process at least twice daily.

4. On the third day (depending on the temperature) the seed should be sprouted enough to feed to the birds.

5. The sprouted seed is then rinsed clean and then soaked in a disinfectant (Aviclens by Vetafarm, a household bleach diluted 1:100 etc.) for twelve minutes before the final rinse. Aviclens (chlorhexidine) may be safely used in the water during the complete process whereas a bleach can only be used for the final rinse. Aviclens is recommended in all stages with the sprouting of suspect or untested seeds.

6. The unused sprouted seed should be discarded after twelve hours.

Precautions

There are dangers of infecting both the parents and especially the young nestlings when improper sprouting technique is used.

The Gouldian Finch is particularly sensitive to contaminated sprouts and illness associated with improper sprouting shows as infertility, abandoning the nest (eggs or babies), dying 1-3 day old nestlings, poor development in older nestlings, ill or dying parents. There is usually a tail bob and pasted vents in adults suffering from a sprout related illness. Other non specific signs of illness in adults and poor thrift in the youngsters may occur.

The breeding performance of an aviary is improved with the proper use of sprouts however, when improperly used sprouts can be a major and frustrating cause of breeding failure. Seed cleanliness and quality together with good hygiene guarantee the successful use of sprouts.

Symptoms of Disease Related to Poor Sprouting Hygiene

Non-specific illness in adult breeding season associated with:-

1. Sudden deaths of nestlings of any age with a full crop.

2. During the breeding season all of the babies may die suddenly with a full crop at any age, and usually without infertility or dead in shell problems.

Food and Water Management

Food and water containers are especially prone to contamination by harmful bacteria and fungi. Warm weather accelerates the multiplication of these dangerous disease forming organisms and the summer months of breeding make young birds especially prone.

Water contamination is an important source of danger to the Gouldian Finch.

Water borne bacteria such as E. Coli, Klebsiella, Pseudomonas and Citrobacter are the main culprits of bacterial induced problems in the Gouldian Finch. With persistent reinfection of Gouldians the water must first be investigated. The problem is further exacerbated if containers are placed under perches.

Symptoms of Poor Water and Food Management

Non specific symptoms at any time of year associated with:-

1. Recurring illness after the use of appropriate medication in birds of all ages and both sexes.

Diseases Related to Bad Hygiene in the Aviary

The first signs of disease relating to bad hygiene may at first appear as a minor problem with one or two adult birds dying suddenly in the non breeding season.

Thereafter, if the disease is not identified, the occasional adult will die after a short non specific illness with the major signs being lethargy, the fluffed up appearance typical of an ill finch, a pasted vent and often a tail bob indicating respiratory involvement. There may then be no deaths until a stress period (such as a cold spell, moulting or breeding) occurs.

Bacteria and fungi are the major causes of illness due to bad hygiene and have their major effect on the breeding success in the Gouldian aviary. The diseases do not always noticeably affect the adult bird and many birds become "carriers" of these diseases. A "carrier" bird is one which appears healthy but is capable of infecting other birds under certain conditions. Such conditions occur during the stress times of the finch's life i.e. the breeding season and the moulting season, the active developmental stages of the finch embryo inside the egg as well as the growing nestling, the weanling and fledgling.

Infections related to bad hygiene may appear at first as infertile eggs or as many eggs failing to hatch. Certainly infertile eggs early in the season is commonplace, however high numbers of "dead in shell" indicates a problem with the nutrition (i.e. low protein diet etc.) or disease related to bad hygiene. The diagnosis of the problem is made by analyzing the eggs which fail to hatch.

Deaths of 1 to 3 day old nestlings is a common problem with Gouldians and the cause is due to one of many infections rather than to the poor parenting qualities of the Gouldian. The diseases related to bad hygiene are a cause of such early deaths as well as mortality in nestlings at the pin feather stage (about 10 to 14 days of age).

Illness or a few deaths of weanlings and fledglings may occur as the juveniles are transferred from the breeding aviary to the "holding" aviary. An informed disease preventative programme together with a good hygiene can cure these unwell birds.

Survival of the fittest may produce a hardy bird however those fortunate juvenile Gouldians which survive the infections related to bad hygiene do not necessarily produce healthy youngsters. It is necessary to identify the disease(s) involved in the aviary and then to rectify those areas of management which may be causing the disease(s). The appropriate antibiotic can be used at critical times in the breeding cycle to good effect after the management flaw has been rectified. The best time for a short five day course of antibiotics is two weeks before pairing, whilst sitting on eggs and at the first signs of nestling illness or death. The early signs of illness in Gouldian nestlings may be a redness to the skin and retarded growth (see photograph page 56).

Symptoms of Disease Related to Bad Hygiene in the Aviary

Illness and deaths of birds in all seasons and especially associated with:-

1. Poor breeding performance, including infertility, dead in shell and dying nestlings.
2. Illness at fledgling.
3. Illness and deaths during the first moult.

Appropriate Quarantine

The most common cause of disease in the healthy and successful breeding Gouldian aviary is by the introduction of new stock which have not been properly quarantined.

Unfortunately, the quarantine process does not prevent the entry of all diseases and it is recommended that new Gouldian stock be bred in isolation for one season. Any disease undetected during the quarantine stay will surface during the breeding season and the resident flock will be protected and remain healthy and productive.

One main sign of a quarantine problem is an illness in either a resident bird or in a new bird which occurs within three weeks of the introduction. The symptoms associated with the illness vary according to the disease(s) involved.

The ill birds are isolated immediately and the illness diagnosed. The rest of the flock is medicated appropriately on a preventative programme, whilst the ill birds are treated in isolation. Disinfections are used to lower the degree of contamination within the aviary. The best broad spectrum disinfectant for finches is a chlorine based one such as household bleach (dilute 1:100) or Halamid (3gms per litre).

It must be noted that it is not necessarily the introduced bird which is the source of infection. A veterinary examination will determine which bird is a "carrier". Often perfectly healthy Gouldian Finches will become infected after being introduced to a new aviary and the "new bird" is not a "carrier" of disease. The signs of illness in such a situation will occur from one week to six months after the introduction occurs.

Symptoms of Disease Associated with Improper Quarantine

Illnesses (the signs of such vary according to the disease involved) associated with:-

1. A resident exposed recently to an introduced bird (less than three weeks)
2. A new bird recently introduced (less than three weeks).
3. A new bird exposed to an infective resident flock (one week to six months after its introduced.

Nutritional Aspects of Disease

The main signs of poor nutrition for the Gouldian Finch appear most commonly during the breeding and moulting seasons.

Poor fertility, dead in shell, poor parenting, fledgling illness and illness of juveniles during the first moult should alert the informed aviculturist to consider poor nutrition as cause of the problem.

Although the appropriate balance of foodstuffs may be given to the aviary, it must be remembered that not always do the birds accept the foods and consume them. Further more, there is no guarantee that the birds will consume the food items in the proper dietary proportions. For this reason the remnants of the seed, soft food mixes and greens should be investigated in order to ascertain the food types being eaten. Remember to place the food on a high bench and not on the floor (especially if it has not previously been fed to the birds).

Gouldian Finches (and other birds) tend to select their foods according to habit (what they are accustomed to eating) and the appearance of the foods offered. The presentation of new food items is particularly important for the Gouldian. Large pieces of cuttle bone will lie dormant for years in a Gouldian aviary whereas breaking it in to smaller pieces will attract the inquisitive Gouldian. The soft food mix and sprouts provided by John Sammut are visually attractive to the Gouldian and the "soft food" rack attached to the side of the cage makes sense from a hygiene and avicultural point of view.

Symptoms of Disease Associated with Poor Nutrition

Non-specific signs of illness occurring in the breeding and moulting seasons associated with:-

1. Infertility
2. Dead in shell
3. Dying nestlings
4. Nest abandonment
5. Incomplete moult and poor feather quality
6. Small sized progeny

Rodent and Insect Control

Mice and other rodents in the Gouldian aviary are a major cause of disease to finches of all ages.

Mice transmit a bacterial disease which causes sudden illness and deaths especially seen in Winter during cold wet spells. The mice contaminate the food both in the aviary and in the feed storage areas. The effective control of this bacterial disease relies both on the use of the appropriate antibiotics (e.g. Sulfa drugs) and the elimination of the rodent problem by proper seed storage and bates etc.

Insects, slugs, snails and other bugs are a potential hazard to the health of the Gouldian Finch.

Not only o they transmit the tapeworm to the finch, but they also act as transport agents (fomites) of bacteria and other diseases. Eranol⁽ᵀ⁾ is safely used by most serious Gouldian breeders to kill insects in the seed. The snails etc are prevented by good hygienic management procedures. (i.e. The regular removal of wasted dry food and vegetable matter etc.)

Tapeworms cause mortality in all ages of Gouldians and are a more common problem in the warmer Summer months when the insect host is prevalent.

The control of tapeworms rests with insect control and the preventative use of Droncit⁽ᵀ⁾ in the dry food mix. Droncit 10mg should be given in the soft food at the rate of approximately 1 tablet per 2.5kg of bird body weight. So to estimate the dose, calculate the weight of finches to be treated ie. 50 finches @ 20g = 1000g of finches. Then estimate how much soft food they eat in one day eg. 200g. At 1 tablet per 2.5kg, 1000g of finches would approximately require 0.5 tablet to 200g of soft food.

The main symptoms of rodent related disease is a pasted vent, lethargy and the sudden death of one or two adult birds. In the breeding season the hen birds will more commonly be affected whereas in the non-breeding season the cock birds will become ill. Think of these bacterial diseases if after a cold spell or during winter there are deaths of adult birds and there are mice droppings visible in the aviary or food storage area.

The best treatment for rodents is a product called Quinone⁽ᵀ⁾ (a gaseous fumicide safe to birds).

Predators such as Butcher Birds, Currawongs or cats are a source of considerable stress to the Gouldian and must be prevented from climbing on the top of the aviary.

The main signs of predator related stress are nervous birds, failure to nest build, infertility, dead in shell (because of poor brooding activity) and abandonment of the nestlings. The adult birds may also develop bacterial infections causing diarrhea and sometimes death due to septicaemia. Observation of the aviary from a distance is a necessary part of predator control.

Informed Use of Medications

The inappropriate use and over use of medications is a common cause of continuing illness in the Gouldian aviary. The aim of every aviculturist is to produce a hardy, healthy and disease resistant bird which will thrive in an aviary under good management conditions. Constant or irregular use of antibiotics and other medications lower the natural resistance of all birds, especially the Gouldian, which in the long term renders the bird unable to repel infection by its natural immunity. The end result is a bird which is susceptible to all types of disease.

The use of the "sulfa" family of antibiotics is preferred to the tetracyclines as the first line of defence against an outbreak of illness in the Gouldian aviary.

In my opinion, the tetracyclines (Oxy-B, Chlortetracycline and Doxycycline) should be used only when Chlamydiosis has been identified. The disease is very uncommon in Gouldians.

Symptoms of Disease Associated with the Improper Use of Medication

Recurring illness at any time of the year in all ages and in both sexes of Gouldians associated with:-

1. The incorrect and inappropriate antibiotic (e.g. Tetracyclines)
2. The continual use of medications (e.g. Ronidazole etc.)

Temperature Control

Disease in the Gouldian aviary can be controlled by understanding that "stress" is the basis of all illness. Stress is anything which upsets the birds normal a routine.

The sudden fluctuation of temperature is of particular concern for the Gouldian Finch and the temperature within the aviary must be controlled (by insulation or thermostatic heaters) for successful breeding.

Poor breeding results may reflect incorrect temperature control.

Foster Parents

Some breeders of the colour mutations of the Gouldian Finches use Bengalese finches as foster parents. The Gouldian Finch is a prolific egg layer but often a poor parent. The Bengalese finch is chosen as the foster parent because it is a good feeder and resistant to disease.

Foster parents can be used to advantage with normal Gouldians in an aviary with Air Sac mite.

The life cycle of the Air Sac mite is broken by using the resistant Bengalese as foster parents. In normal circumstances the entire life cycle of this mite is spent in the respiratory membranes, and the mites are transmitted directly to the nestlings or between adults via contamination of food and water from coughing and sneezing. The Air Sac mite is much more serious in the Gouldian finch than the resistant Bengalese Finch. The life cycle is interrupted successfully by using Bengalese as foster parents and not exposing the young fledgling Gouldians to the

1 - Bengalese used as foster parents will break the cycle of the air-sac mite.

1 - DR ROB MARSHALL

adult Gouldians of the Air Sac mite infested aviary. The adult infected Gouldians may be successfully treated using Ivermectin. Ivermectin is used at the dose of 4 micrograms per bird given as a "spot-on" treatment to the skin of the chest once a week for 4 weeks. The Ivermectin is diluted with sterile water or propylene glycol and available by prescription only.

Bengalese Finches are sometimes dangerous to the health of nestling Gouldians.

Bengalese Finches are extremely hardy and resistant to diseases to which the Gouldian nestlings are highly sensitive. It is extremely important to select perfectly healthy Bengalese as foster parents. Ideally a veterinary examination of the droppings of the Bengalese is preferred before they are used as foster parents for the colour mutation Gouldians. The Bengalese Finches may appear extremely healthy to the naked eye but in fact be "carriers" of disease which may infect the Gouldian Finch. The most common diseases "carried" by the Bengalese which are lethal to the nestling Gouldians are the gram negative bacterial diseases, Campylobacteriosis, Cochlosomiosis (Bowel parasite) and Papovavirus.

The "Carrier Bird"

The "Carrier Bird" is one which appears healthy but is capable of infecting other birds (i.e. it carries disease) and itself may become ill or die under times of stress.

A "carrier" bird can only be detected by special tests performed by an avian veterinarian. The "carrier" bird concept applies more so to the Bengalese foster parent than to the Gouldian parent during the breeding season. However at other times of the year and especially during the juvenile moult the converse is true.

Symptoms of Diseases Related to a "Carrier Bird"

Non-specific illness of adult birds in the breeding and moulting season associated with:-
1. Sudden deaths in nestlings
2. Illness in fledglings
3. Illness during the juvenile moult
4. The disappearance of illness outside these stress periods
5. Healthy Bengalese adults and Bengalese nestlings

Gouldians in a Mixed Aviary

There are many different species of finch and over the years in the wild they have adapted to differing and special requirements for their survival and procreation. The Gouldian Finch appears to have adapted in an environment relatively free of disease. Phylogenetically it has become a bird susceptible to certain diseases in the aviary situation. For this reason Gouldians kept in mixed aviaries are at the greatest risk to illness compared to the other finch species.

Gouldians from a veterinary point of view should not be housed with other bird species.

However, this may not be a satisfactory statement from an aviculturist's point of view and the following notes may help the aviculturist choose which bird species may offer the best chance for the Gouldian's survival in the mixed aviary.

The Parrot Finch is thought to be the closest relative of the Gouldian finch and for this reason may be the most suited finch species to mix with the Gouldian from a disease point of view.

A mixed collection of other peaceful finch species is certainly

1 - The Parrot Finch is regarded as the most suitable species to mix with Gouldians.

1 - DR ROB MARSHALL

more satisfactory than say a mixed parrot and finch collection.

The small Neophema Parrots and quiet Princess Parrots would be a suitable combination in the mixed aviary if parrots had to be the choice. The Gouldian Finch is easily stressed psychologically when mixed with aggressive species such as the Red-rumps or Rosellas etc. Gouldians should not be mixed with Budgerigars.

Some mixed aviaries may have existed without any problems for years and you may question the worth of this material. However, the chances of maintaining the health of a Gouldian Finch in a mixed aviary is considerably lessened by the following situations in increasing order of risk.

1. Gouldians with Parrot Finches
2. Gouldians with Australian finches
3. Gouldians with non-Australian finches
4. Gouldians with Neophemas
5. Gouldians with Princess
6. Gouldians with Budgies
7. Gouldians with Rosellas, Red-rumps, etc.
8. Gouldians with Quail
9. Gouldians with Doves or Pigeons
10. Gouldians with Guinea Pigs or Rabbits.

Groupings 1-5 are acceptable combinations in the non-breeding ornamental aviary, whereas Groupings 6-10 are totally unacceptable combinations for the continuing health of the Gouldian anywhere.

Symptoms of Diseases Associated with a Mixed Aviary

Illness and deaths occurring in Gouldians associated with:-
1. No deaths or illness in other species.

Overcrowding

Overcrowding in Gouldians is a most common cause of potential disease problems.

It creates both a physical and psychological stress to this and all other bird species. John Sammut has recommended that no more than 2-3 pairs of breeding Gouldians be housed together in a breeding aviary (3 metres (9ft 6in) x 1 metre (3ft) x 2.1 (6ft 8in) metres high) and that the number of juveniles be restricted to 12 in a holding cage (6 feet x 18 inches x 15 inches).

The overcrowded aviary creates more competition for food

Page 73

and water sites, perch sites and nesting sites. As well as considerable psychological trauma to the Gouldian. The physical and psychological stresses caused by overcrowding renders the immune system of the Gouldian incompetent and predisposes the flock to illness.

1 - DR ROB MARSHALL

Recognition of Disease

Symptoms of Diseases Associated with Over Crowding
Signs of non-specific illness and deaths associated with:-
1. Recurring disease outbreaks after the appropriate use of medications.

Early recognition of disease is extremely important if these diseases are to be controlled.

Because birds have the great ability to hide their illnesses, any bird that appears sick must be helped immediately.

Good aviary management must include a proper surveillance of the flock for signs of illness. Signs of an unwell bird are sometimes subtle, however with careful observation they will become very clear and alert you to take immediate first aid steps. It is best to observe the birds from a distance before more closely observing the flock. This way it is possible to see how the birds are behaving in their undisturbed environment and any abnormal behaviour can be more accurately determined.

Recognising a healthy bird allows us to be able to detect a bird which is unwell.

So, it is important to observe your birds and get to know their normal behavioural patterns.

The signs of illness vary according to the disease involved, but initially there are some general changes which occur in the ill bird.

1. Any Change in a Bird's Normal Behavioural Pattern
The bird is less active than normal, fluffed up with both feet on the perch, rubbing its head on the perch, has a slight tail bob, its head behind its wing, sitting low on the perch or appears sleepy.

2. Any Change in the Bird's Physical Appearance

1 - Overcrowding causes stress which triggers disease. Avoid overcrowding your birds.

The bird may sneeze, have wet feathers around the head, have a wet eye, have an eye shut, a droopy wing, faeces stuck to the vent or tail feathers or be unable to fly.

Once recognised as being ill the Gouldian should be moved to a specially designed hospital cage which should be away from the aviary.

This cage provides an opportunity for the bird to rest in a controlled environment, isolates the bird from the rest of the aviary and allows you to more closely observe the bird and to start any intensive treatment which may be necessary.

It is necessary to place the ill bird under the least amount of stress as possible.

The birds should be held as little as possible and then placed into the prepared hospital cage. The cage and feed/water containers should be already disinfected, filled with fresh food and water and a piece of clean newspaper or gladwrap placed on the floor in order to collect fresh dropping samples for analysis. Elevated water and food containers are preferred. "Tasty" sprouted seed may stimulate the ill Gouldian to eat.

Examine the bird carefully before placing it into the warmed hospital cage. Write down the findings of this examination noting any symptoms such as weight loss (going light), pasted vent, watery eyes, color of the dropping etc. which may help the veterinarian make his diagnosis. Provide a quiet environment etc.

Provide controlled heat at about 30 degrees Celsius. Observe that the bird is eating and collect a dropping. Phone your avian veterinarian for advice. He may recommend some immediate therapy whilst the droppings are analysed.

It is important to collect a fresh dropping and wrap it in an air tight manner before any medication is given. It is difficult to identify many diseases once medication has been given.

If the bird is not eating or has not eaten, force feeding may be necessary. With the Gouldian a small crop needle can be used to good effect. Fluids are a very important part of treatment. Keep food and water in easy reach. Move the food and rearrange the perches so that the food is constantly in front of the bird.

Without food the ill birds body temperature drops rapidly and without water dehydration occurs.

It is a good idea to learn a forcefeeding technique utilizing a crop needle. Most bird clubs have demonstrations on these techniques. A good energy mix for the ill bird is glucose and water (1/4 teaspoon of Glucodin powder to 30mls of water) given warm by crop needle or placed in the water dish. This solution must be made fresh and replaced within 12 hours.

Do not give medication such as antibiotics which may interfere with the diagnostic tests.

After a dropping has been collected use a sulfa drug such as Sulfa D$^{(T)}$ as the first line of medication.

A quick accurate diagnosis is essential if the bird patient is to be saved. The diagnosis of most bird conditions can be made more quickly now that there are reliable diagnostic procedures available (e.g. blood tests, bacterial culture and special stains used on body fluids.) However, an accurate diagnosis can be made difficult, if incorrect first aid treatment is given before the veterinarian is consulted.

To get the best out of your avian veterinarian follow the guidelines below.

The flock-health takes precedence over the health of the individual in the aviary bird situation and sometimes, sad as it may seem it becomes necessary to sacrifice the life of one ill bird in order to save the rest of the flock.

1. First Assess your Disease Situation

In Gouldian Finches when even one bird falls ill then it may be a threat to your aviary. (This is not necessarily so with other species of finch or parrots). Immediately isolate the ill birds and treat them with appropriate first aid. Contact your avian veterinarian for further advice. Ill birds should be submitted as soon as possible to the veterinarian for immediate analysis.

2. Submit Appropriate Birds to the Avian Veterinarian

To expedite the correct diagnosis it is imperative that ill or dead birds taken for analysis have not been treated with any medication. Most tests for bacterial infections will be erroneous if medications are given within 48 hours of testing.

It is best to submit an ill live bird to the veterinarian so that he can observe the symptoms and take tests in the live bird. Some diseases are difficult to detect in the dead bird and it may be necessary to examine body fluids from the live bird for accurate diagnosis.

Place clean newspaper or gladwrap on the floor of the transport cage of the ill bird so that droppings can be collected and tested immediately on arrival at the veterinary hospital.

Autopsy cannot help in making a correct diagnosis if the bird has been dead more than six hours before it is discovered in the aviary or hospital cage. Gouldian Finches deteriorate very quickly after death and it is important to preserve them as soon after death as possible.

The dead bird must be cooled if the organs are to be preserved for autopsy. This is best achieved by wetting the bird in detergent (to stop the feathers from insulating the body), wrapping the body in paper and then plastic and refrigerating until the body can be taken to the veterinarian. The body is best stored in the vegetable crisper part of the fridge if you are able to get to the veterinarian within 1 day and if it is longer than this time then it is best to place it in the freezer section.

Transport the body to the veterinarian in a cooler.

A detailed autopsy is sometimes the only way of diagnosing a disease in the aviary. Only a few conditions can be accurately diagnosed at autopsy by looking at the organs alone and it is for this reason that detailed autopsy is usually required for the exact diagnosis. A detailed autopsy involves taking tests of the body fluids which will give an immediate recommendation for further first aid treatment. For the exact treatment recommendations the organs must be sent to an avian pathologist for microscopic analysis, with the results back in about 48 hours.

Prevention of Disease in the Gouldian Aviary

Good management prevents disease within the Gouldian Finch aviary. Good management takes into account the system of housing and quarantine, aviary hygiene, proper nutrition, accurate record keeping and an informed policy against disease. By providing the best physical and psychological environment for the Gouldian, breeding results are maximised and diseases minimised. The housing system, quarantine facility, aviary hygiene, nutrition and record keeping have been well covered. I will discuss the disease which most commonly occur within the Gouldian aviary in the management section.

Disease prevention programmes are discussed with special reference to the juvenile bird, the breeding bird, moulting bird and the newly purchased Gouldian Finch.

Disease Prevention in the Off Season

Illness which occurs during the off season ("austere" period) when the natural stresses of the Gouldian Finch are minimal reflects a problem with aviary management.

Immediate steps to identify and rectify the management error must be taken to prevent the disease from affecting the whole flock. The occasional death at this time can be explained by non-infectious causes such as injury and parasites (notably tapeworm).

The Off-season preventative programme includes:-

1. Nutrition

i. A minimal seed diet. Do not feed black (oil seeds) confine the seed mix to millets and canary.

ii. Do not feed sprouts nor soft food mix as these are not needed and produce obesity. The fat Gouldian is a poor breeder.

iii. Give seeding grasses and greens for one day twice weekly. Be careful to remove greens from the aviary the same day to prevent spoilage.

iv. Maintain the charcoal, grit and calcium on a regular basis.

2. Aviary Management

The Gouldian Finch in the off season is susceptible to sudden fluctuations in temperature especially in the cool, wet months of winter. Pay special attention at this time to rodent and slug control, moisture and mould growth in the aviary.

3. Medications

There should be no need to medicate with any antibiotics or anti-protozoals during the off season. For one day a week multivitamin mixture can be added to the water.

Disease Prevention for the Breeding Season

1. Medicate four weeks before pairing

Gouldians should be wormed for tapeworms and the aviary and seed treated for insects (cockroaches, ants, weevils, moths) and slugs at least four weeks before pairing begins. Use either Oxfendazole or Droncit for the tapeworms and Coopex for the insects.

Emtryl or other medications used against the Motile Protozoa (Cochlosoma) should be used for five days at this time as a "cleanser" to the breeding birds. If an outbreak of Cochlosoma occurs during the breeding season, then a continual course of Ronidazole (Ronivet-S) may be necessary so as not to affect fertility. Cochlosoma disease will only be controlled and not eradicated by the use of drugs. Eradication can only be achieved by breeding Cochlosoma resistant Gouldians in a well managed aviary. Medications against Cochlosoma prevents the natural resistance from developing and therefore the continual use of a "control" dose of medication is necessary to prevent continuing outbreaks of this disease during the active breeding season.

Breeding records help to identify those birds which may have a low resistance to Cochlosoma (i.e. illness as fledglings). Treatment of these adult birds before the breeding season and swapping pairs will help to identify and eliminate the "carrier" individuals from your breeding programme.

The "carrier" birds may alternatively be identified by the avian veterinarian. This is done during or immediately after the breeding eason rather than in the off season.

The bacterial diseases are usually food or water related and for this reason can be well managed by good hygiene.

There are some bacterial infections however which may require antibiotics before or during the breeding season when veterinary help is not a practical solution. The antibiotics of most benefit are the sulfa-drugs. These are best given for five days before pairing and then again for five days after egg laying is complete. Water hygiene is very important with bacterial diseases and disinfectants such as chlorhexidine (e.g. Aviclens) can be used before and during the breeding season on a continual basis without ill effect to the babies or parents. Remember, however, that antibiotics and disinfectants is the simple cure, but masks the presence of illness and susceptibility to disease in the Gouldian. It is impossible to develop a disease resistant Gouldian breeding flock whilst the birds are on medication.

2. Nutrition

The Gouldian Finch must be prepared for the breeding season some six weeks before pairing.

This is outlined in the avicultural part of this book. A disease prevention programme is best given before the breeding season in an aviary where breeding problems have previously occurred.

3. Aviary Management

The most common diseases of the breeding season are the bacterial diseases, Campy liobactercosis, yeast, Cochlosomosis and Papovavirus. All of these diseases can be said to be "stress oriented". The stress involved relates mostly to food hygiene and "carrier" birds.

"Carrier" birds are difficult to detect without veterinary help, however, the danger of the "carrier" bird is considerably lessened if the aviary (habitat) conditions are considered optimal.

Special attention is given to the birds during the six week "flushing" diet.

The birds are observed very carefully for signs of a quick response to the improved quality of feeding. Those birds which are slow to respond to the call of breeding must be more closely observed for signs of "unwellness". These birds may in fact be "carriers". It is good policy to house those "vital" pairs in the one aviary and those less active pairs in a different aviary. This separates the potential dangers of the suspect "carriers" from the most vital (and possibly most disease resistant) individuals in the breeding aviary. The aim of the Gouldian breeder should be to breed a disease resistant Gouldian Finch.

Food hygiene in these six weeks before the breeding season is especially important. Bad habits developed at this time will carry over to the breeding season. It is necessary to get into the correct routine with soft food and sprouting preparation. 3 weeks after pairing, samples of the soft food, sprouts and droppings from the breeding pairs can be submitted to an avian veterinarian for analysis. It is best to understand and rectify any problems before the birds go to nest.

Papovavirus is the most frustrating of all the Gouldian diseases.

It reflects a lowered immunity in the finch and is usually associated with other infections. Papovavirus can only be diagnosed by special pathology tests and the control of the disease requires a knowledgeable avian veterinarian and a patient Gouldian breeder.

Yeast infections in the breeding season cause stunted growth in nestlings and is most often associated with other disease processes.

Chlorhexidine (Aviclens)[T] on a continued basis will control but will not cure the problem. Veterinary help is necessary if this disease is to be completely eradicated. Sometimes bread crumbs and an improperly prepared soft food mix can predispose the breeding Gouldian to this condition. A vitamin A deficiency may also be incriminated as a cause of yeast infections.

Disease Prevention during the Adult Moulting Season

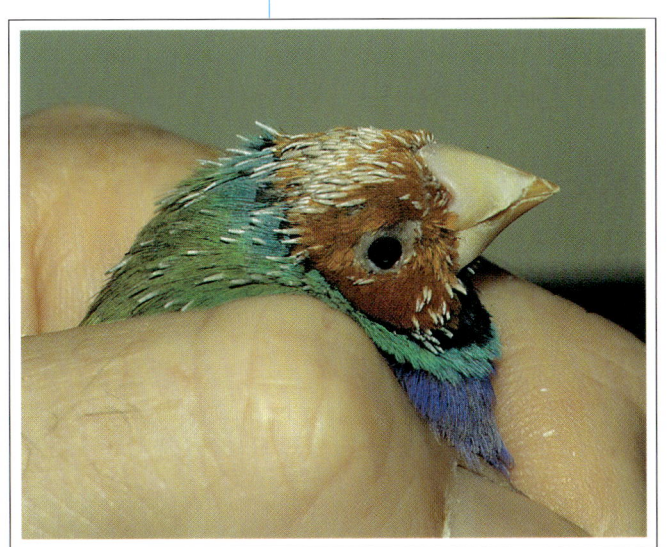

The end of the breeding season signals the beginning of the moulting season.

No medications should be given after the breeding season unless a specific illness has been diagnosed. The adult moult is a significant time of potential illness for the breeding Gouldian. Nature has certainly ensured the "survival of the fittest" by having the moult immediately after the breeding season. The rigours of the breeding season are followed by the protein depleting moult. The necessary high protein requirements of replacing every feather on the body means there must be an available protein source. The plethora of insect life and the remaining seeding grasses in the wild provide the necessary protein for the moulting season. In the aviary situation the required protein intake is paramount if the moult is to be successfully completed.

Birds "stuck in the moult" could also be due to an inadequate level of dietary intake of protein, a problem with the absorption of protein from the bowel (e.g. Bowel infections or vitamins deficiencies) or a cold spell before the moult is complete. Birds are especially susceptible to illness during the moult and it is important not to add any further burden to the Gouldian at this time. All medications are with-held and there is very careful aviary management. The diet is fortified with seeding grasses, soft food mix high in egg content and a high black seed (niger, rape, lettuce) diet. The percentage of these black seed should not exceed 5% in total. A good varied mix of millets and other small seeds ensures a well balanced amino acid balance to the dietary protein.

1 - DR ROB MARSHALL

1 - This Gouldian is "stuck in the moult". There are a number of causes.

Medication after the Adult Moult

The time to give a preventative disease programme is after the adult moult is completed. This programme starts three weeks after all of the primary flights and tail feathers have been replaced by healthy new feathers.

The medications given now prepare the Gouldian for the following breeding season. Tapeworm and Gizzard worm treatment is given if these have been a problem in the past. Gizzard worm is a particularly difficult worm to treat and usually is associated with an insect intermediate host. Gouldian breeders who feed mealworm must give medications at this time for worms. Use Nilverm for the Gizzard worm and Droncit(T) for the tapeworm. A repeat treatment of Nilverm is given three weeks later and every effort is taken to identify and eradicate the intermediate host.

Two weeks after worming a Sulfa drug is given for five days to "re-sterilize" the bowel. The healthy finch has no bacteria in the bowel. A multivitamin is then given daily for one week in the drinking water, after which a disinfectant such as Chlorhexidine (Aviclens)(T) is given daily in the water for three weeks.

Disease Prevention during the Juvenile Moult

The juvenile moult represents a totally different scenario as compared to the adult moult. Both are extremely difficult times for the Gouldian, however, the adult bird has the advantage of a competent and mature immune system. This renders the adult more capable of repelling illness. The juvenile Gouldian has a low resistance to disease from the fledgling age to the completion of its first moult. It is during this time that most illnesses occur in the Gouldian. Medications in certain circumstances play an important part in producing the final product i.e. a fully colored Gouldian on the perch. The juvenile Gouldian is much less of a health risk after the completion of the first moult and the ppropriate use of medication helps to hurdle the dangers of this difficult time.

A similar high protein diet as fed during the adult moult is given to the moulting juveniles. The major problems of the juvenile moult tend to be yeast, bacterial, motile and non-motile protozoal infections. The use of Chlorhexidrine (Aviclens)(T) on a permanent daily basis during this time would be a recommended procedure in a Gouldian flock which has experienced problems at this time in the past (however, I would not recommend the use of any disinfectant in a healthy Gouldian flock which has not experienced past problems.) As stated previously the aim is to develop a disease resistant flock in a "natural" manner. The immune system functions better and in a more complete manner when there are no additives in the water.

Sulfaquinoxaline should be used in cases where overcrowding occurs. Protozoal infections of juveniles are common. Atoxoplasmosis occurs as an intestinal disease more so than the more common liver/spleen disease as seen in canaries. The treatment with Sulfaquinoxaline for five days of each week until the moult is completed will help control Atoxoplasmosis. Sometimes other Sulfa combination drugs may be necessary.

Cochlosomosis is caused by a flagellate, Cochlosoma which lives happily in the intestinal tract of Bengalese, is a common cause of illness in young Gouldian female from the age of six weeks till after moulting. The typical signs are debilitation, shrivelling and staining yellow of the fledglings, difficulties with the moult and undigested seed seen in the droppings. Treatment of this disease is with Ronidazole (Ronivet-S) the dose of 400mg/kg egg food and 400mg/litre of drinking water for five days per week. This drug is safer than Dimetridazole (Emtryl)[T].

Preventative Programme for Fledglings

Fledgling occurs about 24-26 days of age in healthy Gouldians. The fledglings are moved from the parents into a holding cage two to three weeks later. Fledgling and weaning is a stressful time for Gouldian finches and a time at which illness may occur. I would recommend Levamisole Nilverm) 25mls /litre of drinking water to the birds in the breeding aviary two weeks after fledgling occurs. This is repeated for one day each month for three months to the juveniles as an immune stimulant and to help control gizzard worm problems.

Ronidazole (Ronivet) is given to the breeding aviary at fledgling time only if a previous Cochlosoma problem has been diagnosed. Ronidazole which is given to a flock without previous Cochlosomosis problems may in fact precipitate an outbreak in the fledglings.

Viral Infections

Papovavirus

Is a breeding disease seen in the Gouldians. It causes death in nestlings, juveniles and adults. The symptoms are not specific and the diagnosis can only be made with special pathology tests.

Paramyxovirus

This is a virus which causes head tilt and head turning (torticollis) in the Gouldian. These birds can be "carriers" for months before signs of the diseases become obvious. This diseases can be confused with Vitamin E deficiency, which is

The more Common Diseases seen in the Gouldian Finch

1 - Healthy fledglings in the moult.

1 - DR ROB MARSHALL

caused by feeding rancid cod-liver oil or mixing oil through the seed. Cod-liver and other oils should be stored in the refrigerator.

Chlamydial Infections

Chlamydiosis (Ornithosis/Psittacosis) is extremely uncommon in Gouldian finches. The signs of this disease are not specific, but include apathy, diarrhea, nostril and eye discharge. The tetracycline drugs are effective at curing this disease but must be given for 30 days. The dose rate is 100mg/litre of drinking water or 1500mg/kg of soft food. The tetracyclines should not be given for any other diseases of Gouldians.

Bacterial Infections

The most common bacterial problems seen in the Gouldian are due to the Enterobacteriacea (E. Coli, Klebsiella and Citrobacter), Pseudotuberculosis, Streptococci and Staphylococci, Pseudomonas and Aeromonas infections and Salmonellosis. The Enterobacteria are usually a result of an unbalanced diet which weakens the birds. The Enterobacteriacea present commonly as a secondary problem E.Coli is a secondary pathogen and is considered as a symptom of a lessened health or hygienic condition. The main causes are poor nutrition, housing and management problems. Other diseases such as Coccidiosis or Atoxoplasmosis may also be involved and must be treated accordingly. Sulfa drugs will improve this condition only temporarily unless the actual cause is identified and eliminated.

Klebsiella

Klebsiella infections are usually related to dirty seed and looks very similar to Salmonella infections. A complete cure can be difficult because of "carrier" birds. "Carrier" birds can be identified by the presence of "dead in shell" problems during the breeding season.

Pseudotuberculosis (Yersinia)

Pseudotuberculosis is always related to mice and often occurs after a cold spell. Treatment is with a broad spectrum antibiotic and the elimination of mice.

Pseudomonas and Aeromonas

Pseudomonas and Aeromonas infections occur when the sprouted seed is incorrectly prepared. Dirty drinking vessels or baths can be a source for the foul smelling diarrhea. The cure includes antibiotic treatment and then eliminating the cause of the problem.

Campylobacter Infections

Campylobacter infections are common to the Gouldians especially when bred in association with the Bengalese finch. The Bengalese are often "carriers" and show no signs of illness. The infection is especially seen in fledglings. The main sign is a yellow coloured dropping and lethargy. Prescription antibiotics are used to treat this disease.

Yeast Infections

Candidiasis:- is especially due to unbalanced diets, poor hygiene and the inappropriate use of antibiotics (especially the Tetracyclines). It is a serious problem in the Gouldian Finch and causes death due to a crop infection in nestlings and fledglings.

In juveniles and adult birds moulting problems and watery droppings are the main signs of the disease. Chlorhexidine is used to control this disease (Aviclens (0.5ml per litre of drinking water)) but eradication requires the identification of the cause of the disease.

Protozoal Infections

Cochlosomosis: - is the most serious protozoal infection of the Gouldian Finch, it is especially a problem in young birds from the age of six weeks until the end of moulting. The main signs of the illness are watery droppings which contain undigested seed, moulting problems and apathy.

Atoxoplasmosis: - is found in juvenile birds and is usually associated with overcrowding and poor hygiene. The main signs are diarrhea and deaths in juvenile birds. The diagnosis of this disease requires special tests at post mortem. The cure for this disease is sometimes difficult, but the first medication to be used should be Sulfaquinoxaline (3mls per litre for five days each week until the birds stop dying).

Coccidiosis: - is confined to ornamental aviaries and is associated with wet weather and dirty floors. The treatment with Sulfaquinoxaline is successful in controlling the outbreak but not in preventing the recurrence of the disease. The diagnosis of Coccidiosis requires testing of the droppings by an avian veterinarian between 2pm and night fall.

Helminth Parasites (Acuaria Skrjabini)

The Gizzard Worm infects the Gouldian Finch and causes a diarrhea containing undigested seed, as well as deaths of moulting juveniles. The treatment is with 80 mg Levamisole per litre of drinking water for three days.

The Tapeworm is more of a problem in the Gouldian Finch than the gizzard worm. Insects most notably, the weevil transmit this worm. Slugs are also thought to be involved in the life cycle of the tapeworm; the signs of tapeworm infestation are usually non-specific or a bloody diarrhea followed quickly by death.

The treatment is with Oxfendazole (10mgs per litre of water) daily for 3 days or Droncit in the dry food mix. The insect (intermediate host) must be eliminated (e.g. Coopex) to prevent the recurrence of the problem.

External Parasites

The Red mite (Dermanyssus galinae) is uncommon in the Gouldian Finch, but severe anemia and death due to these blood sucking mites is possible. Respiratory signs and lethargy, then death are the mains signs of this disease. Treatment with Coopex is quick and effective. The mite is usually only seen at night time.

Air Sac mites (Sternostoma Tracheacolum) This the most common ectoparasite seen in the Gouldian. the life cycle is complicated and the nestlings become infected by parents regurgitating nutrients and mites. The signs of Air Sac mites include a decline in physical condition, open mouth breathing, a clicking respiration, coughing, sneezing and head shaking. Gouldians die from this disease most often due to a pneumonia and it may sometimes be confused with Chlamydia. A drop of 0.01% solution of Ivermectin in Propylene Glycol is given on the bare skin of the breast. The life cycle can be broken by using the Bengalese Finches as foster parents.

Medications

The Gouldian Finch has a very high metabolism and therefore antibiotics and other medications are eliminated very quickly. These drugs should be administered not only in the drinking water but also mixed through the soft or egg food for best results. Antibiotics must be administered for at least seven days. Sometimes it is advisable to use artificial lighting to stimulate a 24 hour drinking pattern, although this change of day-night rhythm will disturb breeding and can induce a moult.

Symptoms and Diseases

There is never one symptom of illness which spells out clearly the disease involved. However, symptoms of illness do help the aviculturist and avian veterinarian form an idea of the type of illness which may be occurring. Early detection of illness by good observation gives us a chance to save the individual bird as well as to prevent the spread of disease to the rest of the flock.

The most common symptom of illness detected by aviculturists in the Gouldian is the sick bird look. (i.e. the fluffed up bird with two feet on the perch). However, earlier signs of illness such as behavioral changes and changes in the nature of the droppings can be detected by careful observation. The expensive mutations of the Gouldians can readily be saved if they are submitted for analysis at these early stages.

The following list of symptoms may help the aviculturist to understand the possible causes of illness in his flock. Subtle changes may be detected by the observant bird keeper before irreversible illness has occurred.

Changes in the Droppings

The dropping of a bird contains a white or clear part (the urine equivalent) and a colored part (the feces equivalent). The normal Gouldian dropping depends upon the diet fed and the aviculturist must observe what is "normal" for his flock. Birds fed high levels of vegetables and soft food will have a more wet dropping than those birds on a seed only diet. The most important observation is a change from the normal nature of the dropping. Changes in color, consistency, number, size or smell may be noticed in a bird which has early signs of illness.

Colour Changes

Green Droppings: - May be due to a diet change to greens, due to a bird eating less, due to diseases such as liver disease (bacterial infections) or due to the inappropriate use of medications especially the tetracycline type antibiotics.

Pale Color Droppings: - Usually indicates that there is an indigestion problem in the area of the stomach (proventriculus) and small intestine. This is commonly related to Campylobacter infection, Cochlosoma infection or Papovirus. Other bacteria such as Staphylococcus and Streptococcus may infect the pancreas causing similar pale color droppings.

White or Creamy Colored Droppings: - This indicates that only the "urine" part of the dropping is being produced. It is a sign that the bird is potentially very seriously ill. It is commonly associated with Septicaemia.

Black Droppings: - Indicates bleeding in the upper bowel. This may be related to gizzard worm, tapeworm or serious bacterial infections of these areas.

Yellow Droppings: - Indicates severe liver disease and usually involves the "urine" part of the dropping. It is associated often with a dark green faecal part of the dropping or blood tinged droppings. It is a very serious sign in the Gouldian finch.

Bloody Droppings: - This is usually due to tapeworms, bacterial infections, over engorging sand, dehydration or starvation.

Undigested Seed in Droppings: - This is usually related to bacterial infections of the bowel, Cochlosomosis, Campylobacteriosis or Gizzard worm.

Brown Droppings: - Is usually related to a bacteria related to poor aviary or water hygiene. There is an offensive odor associated with these droppings. It is sometimes associated with an excessive grit intake.

Red brick droppings: - Is usually related to a change in grit to a red grit.

"Chook" Smelling Droppings: - Is usually a bacteria related to poor water, food or aviary hygiene or Candidiasis related to the improper use of antibiotics.

Watery Droppings: - Occur in any bird with excessive thirst. For example on hot days, or with certain medication. it also occurs with Coccidiosis and Fungal infections. Stress in the aviary will also produce watery droppings.

Droppings Stuck to the Vent: - Indicates an infectious process involving the bowel and is a non-specific sign of illness.

Large Droppings: - Are seen before egg laying and during brooding, or with diseases of the bowel such as Candidiasis or Campylobacter.

Small Droppings: - Are seen in a bird which is eating less.

Fewer Droppings: - Is an indication that the bird is eating less.

Feather Loss

Head and/or Back: - is usually due to overcrowding, incompatible groupings, or related to a microscopic mite.

Around Eyes: - Is usually related to a Conjunctivitis and rubbing the eye. In the Gouldian Conjunctivitis is usually due to bacterial, fungal, blood parasite or mite infection.

Around Mouth: - Is usually related to a thrush infection.

Wing and Tail Feathers: - is usually related to an abnormal moult or due to Papovavirus.

Stuck in the Moult: - Is usually due to a cold spell during the moult, related to a nutritional deficiency or a disease process.

Feet Problem

Biting at Feet: - Is usually related to a fungal, mite infection or a swelling.

Swelling of Toes or Feet: - Is related to mosquito bites, nesting material around toe, injury or ergot poisoning.

Beak Abnormalities: - A deformed or long beak is a sign of malnutrition or liver disease. A pale color of the beak may indicate a vitamin deficiency, blood parasite or Papovavirus.

Lameness: - In the Gouldian is usually injury related.

Eye Discharge: - Is usually accompanied with rubbing of the face on the perch and is a sign of conjunctivitis. This may be due to a generalized bacterial infection, a blood parasite or an injury if it involves only one eye.

Rubbing of the Beak on the Perch: - Is a normal activity in the Gouldian unless it is excessive, when it indicates pain in the sinus (bacterial or fungal infections) or mouth (thrust or bacterial infections)

Breathing Difficulties: - Gaping with a clicking sound usually but not always indicates Air Sac Mite. Other causes may include infections of the throat and respiratory system.

A gurgling sound on breathing indicates a bacterial or thrush infection of the throat and respiratory system.

Coughing or sneezing may indicates a fungal or bacterial infection.

Vomiting: - Usually indicates a crop, stomach, gizzard problems or a poison of some sort. Bacterial infection or Cochlosomosis are commonly involved.

Head Tilt: - Is usually Vitamin E deficiency or due to Paramyxovirus.

Tail Wagging: - Tail wagging is usually constipation. Clean the matted feces from the vent gently with a wet cotton bud.

Excessive Hunger: - usually indicates worms, Coccidiosis or infections of the bowel.

Unable to Fly: - In the Gouldian means a very weak and ill bird usually.

Deaths in the Aviary

Sudden Death of Adults

(i) **During the Off Season:** - This is usually a management problem related to poor hygiene, contaminated food-stuff, tapeworms or trauma. Treat with Chlorhexidine (Aviclens)[T] whilst the problem is analysed by an avian veterinarian.

(ii) **During the Moult:** - This usually indicates a "carrier" bird exposed to stress. The stress is usually related to poor nutrition, improper housing conditions or bad hygiene. The disease is usually a bacteria, but may also be fungal, yeast or viral. The appropriate medication will stop the outbreak, but further outbreaks are likely unless the underlying stress is identified and rectified.

The analysis of the disease by an avian veterinarian will help to identify the error in management. The best first aid treatment is isolation of the ill bird, collect a dropping for analysis, then medicate with a sulfa-drug.

(iii) **During the Breeding Season:** - The "carrier" bird is usually exposed to stressful situation. It is commonly a bacterial problem. The death of females out number that of males. The parents may have previously abandoned the nest or discarded youngsters. A complete analysis by an avian veterinarian is the only way to understand the cause of this problem and then to improve breeding results.

Sudden Death of Nestlings

This a common occurrence in Gouldians and there are several possible disease causes. An avian veterinarian is the only person to solve this riddle. Otherwise try the use of a general disinfectant (e.g. Aviclens) during the breeding season.

Dead in Shell and Infertility

Is commonly a bacterial problem associated with a low level of protein in the breeding ration. Look at the water hygiene and reassess the protein levels in the breeding diet. The bacteria needs then to be identified and treated if the problem is to be totally cured.

Dying Fledglings and Birds During the Moult

Both of these times are extremely stressful to the Gouldian. Assess the hygiene and nutrition during these times. Antibiotics and Anti-protozoal preparations can be used to control the problem.

Going Light

"Going Light" refers to the symptom of progressive weight loss. It means the bird is depleting its body reserves as a source of energy. Such birds are usually not eating well or eating but not absorbing the necessary energy. The causes of going light are many fold, but most commonly it is involved with a slowly progressive disease such as Coccidiosis, Gizzard worms, Tapeworms, Blood Parasites or low grade bacterial infections. A routine de-worming, together with water disinfection would be the first step for a "home-cure".

As in all things prevention is better than cure. Only by paying attention to all levels of bird management can any measure of prevention be realised.

Simply the best publications on pet and aviary birds available...

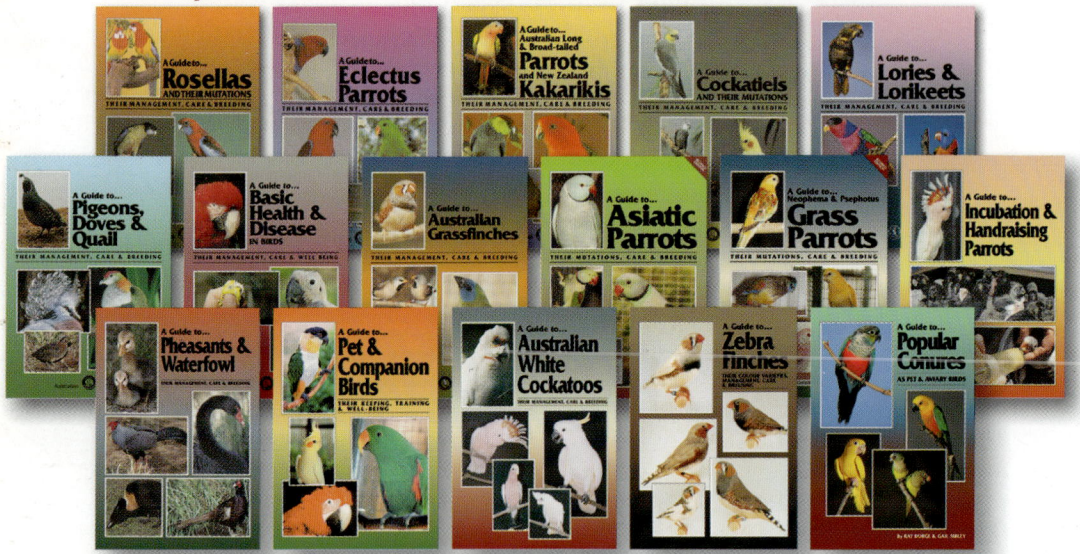

The Acclaimed 'A Guide to' series

Australian BirdKeeper MAGAZINE

Six glossy, colourful and informative issues per year. Featuring articles written by top breeders and avian veterinarians from all over the world.

SUBSCRIPTIONS AVAILABLE
For subscription rates and FREE catalogue contact ABK Publications

Handbook of Birds, Cages & Aviaries

One of the most popular books on the keeping and housing of pet and aviary birds.

For further information or Free Catalogue contact:

ABK PUBLICATIONS

P.O. Box 6288 South Tweed Heads
NSW 2486 Australia

Phone: (07) 5590 7777 Fax: (07) 5590 7130
Email: birdkeeper@birdkeeper.com.au
Website: www.birdkeeper.com.au